THE PPL COMPANION

45 Lessons to Guide You Through Flight Training

DANIEL COLEMAN

First published 2019

Destinworld Publishing Ltd
www.destinworld.com

British Library Cataloguing in Publication Data.
A catalogue record for this book is available from the British Library.

ISBN 9781999647025

Printed and bound in Great Britain by
Marston Book Services Ltd, Oxfordshire

Daniel Coleman was born and raised on the south-east coast of England, in the county of Kent. Having developed an interest in aviation at an early age, he undertook his first flying lesson aged 13. Having completed his A Levels, he joined the Merchant Navy for a short spell, and studied in Southampton. To move towards a career in aviation, he moved back to Kent and, at first, forged a career in logistics while undertaking his PPL flight training. This culminated in the issue of his PPL in August 2018. Daniel now works for a commercial airline based in the Midlands. Besides aviation, Daniel enjoys cooking, playing the piano and reading up on history.

'Armageddon is not around the corner. This is only what the people of violence want us to believe. The complexity and diversity of the world is the hope for the future.'

Sir Michael Palin

CONTENTS

Note – where possible, I have included costs in both British Pound Sterling(£) and Euros(€). However, these exchanges may not reflect the true value as costs and prices vary across the continent and economic region.

Most people's interest in aviation is usually spurred at a young age by an impressive demonstration of flight – by watching in awe as a fighter jet thumps its way through a display at an air show; or by being overwhelmed by the scale of a jumbo jet in amongst the hustle and bustle of a busy international airport. Whatever the tale, everyone has their 'go-to' anecdote, which remains crisp and fresh in their mind and provides the drive for their continued interest in flight. Some people keep their interest purely passive and enjoy aviation through a lens or through keeping up with the latest news and info, which is by no means a negative statement. By nature, aviation enthusiasts are a curious bunch, and I cannot recall a time when I have met an enthusiast who has not dreamt of being behind the controls of a flying machine, however fleeting.

There are many and varied reasons why wannabe pilots walk through the door of a flying club with the goal of achieving their Private Pilot's Licence (PPL). What is important in your journey is to identify the very reason why you plan to do the same. Some prospective pilots have the long-term ambition of flying commercially and view the PPL as purely 'training'; whilst others may have spare time or a general interest in aviation and would very much class the PPL as a hobby – the quintessential weekend pilot!

The beauty of the PPL is that it provides a foundation to branch out in any direction, whatever your intentions are. If your ambition is to work in aviation, either as a pilot or landside, what better way is there to demonstrate your commitment? If your objective is to enjoy flying as a hobby, then the PPL will provide you with the skills to visit new airfields, see the area you live in from above and, of course, impress your family and friends with a seemingly novel trick up your sleeve. Imagine the satisfaction of flying to France for the weekend or across the country for a spot of lunch? Whatever your reason is for showing an interest in learning to fly, the application of the end product spans far and wide .

So, I suppose the first lesson to take away from this book is identify what your motivation to fly is. Jot this down and keep a note of it as, occasionally, you may call this into question. Work out and prepare an answer to this question as I am sure throughout your training and beyond you will be asked this in casual conversation or, perhaps more intimidatingly, whilst in front of an interview panel.

S o, the idea of gaining a PPL has attracted your attention? But how do you go about gaining such a licence to allow you to freely control a heavier-than-air machine across the sky? Well, it will come as no surprise that it will take more than just sending off an application form with a small fee enclosed. Naturally, there is a syllabus that must be completed in order to satisfy a governing authority to grant a PPL.

There are two coveted PPL standards sought by prospective pilots. If you are UK or Europe based, then the EASA (European Aviation Safety Agency) PPL is the syllabus you will need to follow. EASA is an agency of the European Union that acts upon and develops the standards and protocols set by the International Civil Aviation Organisation (ICAO). EASA sets a Europe-wide standard that governs aviation safety and compliance throughout the continent. In addition to member states of the European Union, EASA also grants membership to Norway, Switzerland, Liechtenstein and Iceland. The EASA licence has a standardised syllabus instructed throughout Europe – so you should expect the same quality and depth of training taught in Inverness as is taught in Gdansk.

The EASA syllabus (at the time of writing) consists of a minimum 45 hours' total flight to be made up of:

✈ 25 hours of dual instruction
✈ 10 hours of solo flying, including five hours of solo cross-country flight time, which must also include a cross-country flight that is at least 150NM long and includes visits to two aerodromes.

In addition to the flight time, you must also have:

✈ completed all ground theory examinations, requiring a 75 per cent pass mark.
✈ gained a flight radiotelephony operator licence.
✈ successfully completed a skills test by a certified examiner.

The other favoured syllabus is the FAA PPL, conducted in the USA. The FAA syllabus is broadly similar, covering the same disciplines and techniques; however, it is structured slightly differently. There are two syllabuses – the Part 141 and Part 61, with the former being more rigid and suited to a candidate with professional aspirations, and the latter being less strict and able to be adapted by the instructor. Both syllabuses deliver the student to the same skills test standard. It should be noted that the FAA syllabus requires ground school training tuition to be logged either in the class room or online. For the purpose of this book, my remarks will focus on the Europe-based EASA syllabus.

Of course, geography will naturally dictate the syllabus you will undertake. I have provided a broad overview of the syllabus requirements, but I would strongly advise visiting your country's aviation authority/regulating body website for further clarification. Your chosen flight training organisation will follow the requirements outlined by your country's governing body, but on further research you may (and most likely will) find the way the course is broken down will differ from school to school.

I f you are a relative newcomer to aviation and flight training, I would recommend familiarising yourself with the cost of such an undertaking. Learning to become a pilot is not cheap, and I am not just talking about those pilots who wish to fly commercial airliners. Even a PPL costs a small fortune. Ultimately, I would advise fully briefing yourself with the costs involved. I have witnessed many awkward conversations with passers-by who were visiting the school I trained at enquiring about the cost of training and seeing their gobsmacked faces. Naturally, once met with the answer, these people never return. But, of course, these are not individuals who are seriously looking at gaining a PPL. A good candidate, much like a good pilot, will have fully researched and explored all available resources before reaching out to a training organisation for further pricing details to avoid awkward discussions. With that said, a quick search online will cough out varying figures, but largely a PPL will set you back about £7,000-£10,000 (7,700-11,000 €*).

---

*   Exchange rate £1 = 1.10 € (Winter 2018)

The large variance in price is dependent on a number of factors and does not directly correlate with the quality of training. The price can be influenced by the running cost of the aircraft (aircraft dependent), maintenance and insurance. Other factors to appreciate are instructor pay, economic and geographic region, varying fuel costs and also the understanding that the aircraft may not fly very often, so when they are being used for training the training organisation will be looking to maximise their revenue. On the whole, larger clubs with a busy schedule, swathes of instructors and an ample fleet size will charge a lower 'per hour' rate – a simple economy of scale scenario.

Regarding the 'per hour' rate, a lesson will typically begin with a 30-minute, pre-flight report brief followed by an hour of instruction, and the student should expect to only pay for the time training on the aircraft. Dependent on the aircraft being used for training, an average 'per hour' rate is between £150-£200 (165-220€*) in Western Europe. Other regions in Europe – namely the Eastern parts – tend to be slightly cheaper by comparison.

Beyond the expected hands-on flight training, you must also consider other costs, such as theoretical examinations, the flight radiotelephony operator licence, skills test, medical, landing fees etc, all of which will be discussed further on in this book.

There are two main ways to fund your training and these are either by paying the full cost of the course for a set price up front,

---

*   Exchange rate £1 = 1.10 € (Winter 2018)

if you are able to, or by paying as you go. There are pros and cons to both options. By paying up front you pay a fixed sum to cover the entire cost of training, but with that will come a huge financial and personal commitment to it. If you are on the fence about undertaking the PPL then, perhaps, forking out the full cost of the course up front is not the best course of action. That said, an advantage of paying the cost up front is that you are unlikely to incur any additional costs and, more excitingly, you will be able to move through the syllabus at a swift pace without concerning yourself with how you are going to fund the next lesson. Paying as you go also has its advantages – you are less likely to rush through your training and can spend more time understanding key theoretical principles and airmanship, which may otherwise be crammed in or missed if you are progressing through the training at a faster pace.

When I trained for my PPL, I took the latter option and paid modularly. In retrospect, I feel as though I would have benefitted from saving for several months and, prior to training, paying a larger sum to allow me to progress through the training at a consistent pace. This was a demonstration of a lack of patience on my part as I found the latter part of my training quite fractured in places when I could not afford the next lesson.

The choice of whether to pay up front or as you go is purely a personal one and very understandably circumstantial when assessing the costs involved.

One of the most important decisions you will make will be choosing the training organisation you learn to fly with. Primarily, you will want to choose a school that makes you feel comfortable. That is the most pivotal factor; however, it is also important to be aware of what you are paying for and the value for money you are receiving. Some people are eager to shop around to attain the best value for money, whilst others are happy to take their custom to a school following a recommendation from a friend or family member. In some areas, you may find yourself geographically isolated so the option to 'shop around' may not be available to you.

Two training schools may charge the same 'per hour' rate, but you may end up paying more for your PPL with one school than the other. So, how could it be that you may end up paying more for a PPL at one club than the other, but they seemingly charge the same? Or even worse, you pay less per hour but end up paying more than your friend who is paying more per hour? The answer is likely the landing fees charged.

Some training organisations may charge a landing fee for each landing; for practice take-off and landings (touch and goes) this charge is usually reduced by 50 per cent, broadly speaking. This fee is collected by the flying school on behalf of the air traffic control and airport operator. However, it is not uncommon for landing and touch-and-go fees not to be charged, but this is dependent on the organisation and what agreements they have with the airfield.

A working example:

+ School A charge £150* but charge landing fees of £10 for a landing and £5 per touch-and-go.
+ School B charge a flat rate of £165 and do not charge landing or touch-and-go fees.

You are flying in the circuit and complete seven landings.

+ School A charges £150 + six touch-and-go landings (6 x £5 = £30) + one landing fee at full price (£10), which equates to £190
+ School B charges £165

So, whilst it appears cheaper to fly with school A it may work out cheaper in the long run to fly with school B. Of course, this is a very basic example, but I would highly recommend financial vigilance and astuteness as you move through your training.

---

*   Exchange rate £1 = 1.10 € (Winter 2018)

Many training organisations will offer financial incentives and savings if you deposit a large sum with them. A common incentive I have seen at flying schools is if you deposit £1,000 the club will gift you 5-7 per cent back on your investment – in this example, £50-£70. This would neatly cover a couple of ground theory examinations or several touch-and-go landings, if applicable to that club. Ground theory examinations are another cost you may want to consider when shopping around, as different schools will charge different prices, though largely these will be priced between £25 and £40 each.

It is also worth investigating the membership fees being charged by the clubs you are researching. It is not uncommon to find an organisation that on the face of it appears reasonably priced, especially when reading an attractive 'per hour' rate, to then find they charge £400 a year for membership. If you only fly 25 hours in one year then be sure to factor that extra £16 per flight (£400/25 = £16) on top of the hourly rate.

You will find money haemorrhaging from every angle on the journey to your PPL. Many choose to ignore it, turn a blind eye and accept the costs involved, and if that is you that is fine. But for those who are more cautious and attentive to what they are spending, be sure to note other additional costs such as transport; namely, fuel for your car or public transport. Each time I flew I drove 1.5 hours to the airport and that has an accumulative cost over 50 or so visits. If you are very unlucky you may even be charged for parking at the airfield – I met one pilot during my training who had to pay £5 to park at the airport each time he went flying, the cumulative cost of which would have covered his theory examinations! Though, I would surmise he was one of the unluckier ones or, perhaps, did not care so much.

That said, you would be a fool to select a club purely on its price list as there is more to a club than what it charges: good and bad. Later on in my training, I was offered a job in the aviation sector – an opportunity I could not turn down, so with less than 10 hours of training left to complete on my licence I took a break in my training and moved 200 miles away. After settling in to my new surroundings, I spent some time researching local clubs and took interest in an organisation that was cheaper than my original club. Furthermore, it was only a minute's drive from my work. Without much thought of consequence, I set about contacting my old club and requested they send my training record to my newly sought-out school. Whilst the price was competitive and the location was ideal, I really should have gone for a trial lesson before committing. When I finally flew with them for the first (which also turned out to be the last) time, the aircraft I was assigned to train on had two technical issues, the instruction was far below the standard a student should expect and the club atmosphere was flat and despairing. Whilst cheaper, I felt as though I would have needed to spend double the money I would have otherwise spent at my original club to become familiar with the new area, the instructors and their operation. Naturally, thereafter, I went grovelling back to my original club and continued my training there. A lesson in humility indeed. Although each flight required a 400-mile round trip and the 'per hour' rate was 20 per cent more expensive than at the new club I had found, I felt that returning to my original club was the right decision for my training, and in retrospect I still believe this was the best course of action. I may very well have been put off flying for good had I committed to the new club I had trialled.

As stated at the beginning of this chapter, the most important factor is your comfort at the club. So whilst this is intended to draw your attention towards value for money, good deals and the understanding of pricing, do remember there are other factors that you should evaluate before progressing with the next steps.

With a shortlist of clubs in your local area and a brief understanding of their price list, now would be a great time to visit a couple of clubs and show your face. I am confident if you were to contact a club they would be very receptive and welcoming. As flying is very reliant on fair weather, you may have to wait until a day when the club is in operation – because, of course, you do not want to visit when there is nothing going on as this would not be very insightful. Also, the likelihood is that the club may not even be open, even for administrative tasks or calls, if the weather is not great.

A flying school, depending on its size, can be a busy environment with multiple flights operating simultaneously. In the club house or waiting area there will be students and various people waiting around chatting – so introduce yourself and get involved with the discussion. Some people will be there for the same reason as you, whilst others may be there for a gift experience with their families. Either way, you will find that the conversations will largely be centred around aviation and flying on the whole. Take this opportunity as your first networking opportunity. Your subsequent visits to the school may feel infrequent because of the sometimes seemingly long gaps between your lessons; however, you will likely find the same faces appear when you visit, and again that will be largely attributable to the good weather. So, even at this stage, exchanging names and pleasantries will make your future visits and the long periods you may be waiting around on the ground less awkward and more enriching.

During your visit you will hopefully have the opportunity to meet some of the instructors. During this introduction try to recall the names of the instructors you meet who you feel a good relationship with as this will be important later on when you begin your training. If you do not strike up a positive and relaxed vibe on the ground, then you will not feel particularly comfortable at a later date when that same instructor is throwing instructions and criticisms at you. On the whole, instructors are an approachable bunch. They would not be employed, or instructors, if they did not have that personable appeal.

By this stage, having completed some club research online regarding price list and aircraft fleet, you may have an idea which aircraft you would like to train on. Whilst it is possible to train on multiple aircraft types, I would recommend sticking to one aircraft so you develop a solid, working proficiency on that single aircraft. I have heard of experiences where clubs, on a busy day and if they have overbooked an aircraft, will book low-hour PPL students onto a different aircraft type, which they have not had experience on, to make the flying schedule suit the club. Presumably, this is under the false assumption that a low-hour PPL student would not have gained a high-enough level of proficiency for it to cause disruption to their training. However, I would advise if this happens to you and you are not happy moving onto a different aircraft type, even if it is just for one hour of flying, you are well within your rights to refuse and rebook for a later date. Whilst frustrating, I personally see no point in spending out to suit another party. One could argue it would be another hour in the log book, but I would view it as costing you another hour to re-build proficiency on your chosen aircraft. Later, once you have gained your PPL, transitioning onto a new aircraft will not require much remedial training other than aircraft handling, familiarisation and a check ride with an instructor. But in the early stages of training, transitioning between two aircraft types will not aid your training. At least, that is my opinion anyway.

While at the training club, ask to visit the aircraft. It will provide more context to what being in and around an aircraft will be like. Take the opportunity to visit the aircraft on the ground with an instructor and familiarise yourself with the instruments and controls, though not overly important at this stage, as this will be covered in your training, it may serve as a motivational tool to get you to book that all-important first flight!

I cannot stress enough the importance of visiting a flying school before embarking on flight training. If you gain nothing at all from your visit, at least being familiar with your surroundings will be an advantage to you when you report for your introductory lesson and take flight for the first time.

With some thorough online research conducted and with a visit to a flying club or two, you have finally settled on a training organisation to conduct your training with! Fantastic. This decision can be as short or as long a process as you need or want it to be. But you have made your choice and you should take some pride in the fact that you have made a decision based on informed choices from resources you have sought out. If you have not already been convinced to book a lesson already during a visit, now is the time to book a trial introductory flight.

Booking a trial lesson can be quite a daunting task, though it is much like booking a driving lesson. One calls up the club, queries availability and books a slot. How easy this is and the idea that you are booking a time to fly an aircraft can feel quite novel and surreal at the time. Of course, the first time you book a lesson, either over the phone or in person, you may feel awkward or unsure how to direct the conversation. For the first booking I would recommend just outlining your intention to book a trial lesson around a given date and allow the club's representative to provide you with the information and guide the conversation. If you have any questions, you should feel encouraged to ask them, as the club should hope to dispel any feelings of anxiety or uncertainty on your part. Similar to a driving lesson, you would be expected to pay for your lesson after it is complete. Unless, of course, you decide to deposit a cash amount, whereby the cost of your lesson will be deducted post-flight.

With your first trial flight approaching, to prepare yourself in a way that will see you gain the most from your experience, you may want to consult a variety of online resources to gain a better idea of what to expect.

You may already have a basic understanding of aircraft systems, but it may be a good idea to do some further reading to refresh your knowledge – even if you treat your trial lesson as a sightseeing flight, do not be surprised if you find your instructor asking you questions about the aircraft. This is so they can gauge your level of knowledge and get an impression of your capacity as a student. As your plan is to gain a Private Pilot's Licence, you should have a vested interest in how you present yourself and convey your character. Having some knowledge of the aircraft, and flying as a whole, before climbing into the cockpit for the first time will demonstrate a positive attitude towards learning. Your instructor will surely identify this and adapt their instruction to fit your knowledge but also in a way to challenge you.

I n the days leading up to your first introductory lesson, it would be advisable and in good character to keep an eye on the weather. The key variable you need to look out for at this very early stage in your journey is the wind. For the purpose of an introductory lesson, your instructor will likely keep you in the vicinity of the airfield so the weather of far-flung destinations at this stage is not of much importance. The surface wind on the day will be the stopper to any flying, so in the preceding days keep an eye on this particular weather phenomenon. Though, assuming you have no concept of quantifying and qualifying wind velocity at this stage, having a quick look over the five-day forecast will not do any harm. On the whole, if you hear or read there is a storm arriving around the time of your proposed lesson, it would be safe to say it is likely to be cancelled. However, if you are not of the organised sort then at the very least you should contact the flying club in the morning of your planned flight for a discussion about the weather and the likelihood of the flight going ahead. In the case of obvious inclement weather, any good club would likely contact you before you have the chance to contact them, to delay or reschedule the booking.

For your first introductory lesson, it would be advisable to arrive in good time for a thorough brief and to settle any pre-flight jitter and nerves. Ahead of your brief, speaking to club members or other students in similar straits will go a long way to ease your anxieties ahead of your flight. Whilst on the topic of pre-flight anxieties, I must stress the importance of eating a good meal no less than one hour before stepping foot near that aircraft. It may seem counterintuitive (a common theme in all facets of flight training), but having a meal will help to settle your stomach and reduce the likelihood of you suffering from nausea and motion sickness. In my earlier training I suffered notoriously from motion sickness and nausea; my pre-flight nerves and misplaced belief that having a full stomach would exacerbate the problem invariably exacerbated the problem! Nowadays, a hearty breakfast roll or a cheap meal deal is a seminal part of my pre-departure ritual, and you must not forget the importance of remaining hydrated. Of course, early in your training you will likely experience some discomfort while flying, so experiment with different ways of preparing yourself for flight. It may seem trivial; driving a car requires no prior physiological preparation. However, flying an aircraft, especially for the first time, requires a greater demand mentally. As such, preparing your body for the physical pressures, in turn, takes off some of the mental pressures and will allow you to focus solely on the task of controlling the aircraft. This is not to say you will be pulling excessive positive and negative G forces, but you would be a fool to not expect some mild turbulence while flying. Further to this 'chop', there will also be the subtle vibration of the aircraft's engine reverberating through every surface you are in contact with. Naturally, over time you will learn to ignore these subtle forces. In summary, where possible try to make sure you are physically prepared and rested for flying – more of this later in your ground theory examinations.

You will likely be introduced to your instructor by the club manager or operations co-ordinator that day. As lightly addressed in the previous chapter, your instructor will probe and enquire, in a similar manner to that of a doctor, about your interest in aviation, your experience and understanding of flying. Much of how your flight will pan out will depend largely on your expectation, how you convey this and your instructor's understanding of it. With regards to your experience and understanding, it would be sensible to approach this with honesty (of course why would you lie?) and try to leave any ego or superfluous information at the door. By this I mean by all means tell the instructor if you have watched cockpit videos or have fiddled around with a computer-based flight simulator and recognise some flight instruments...but do not start professing how great you are because you once greased a landing in a Boeing 737 on a grass strip from your desktop computer at home. I realised quickly that these kind of people find themselves in the unenviable position of not being taken particularly seriously. As with any form of training and assessment, any knowledge held in advance can be used to your advantage and will be helpful, but ultimately all the skills and information needed for you to succeed will be taught to you. Or at the very least you will be guided towards them.

Equipped with their understanding of your knowledge and what you want to get out of your introductory lesson, the instructor will brief you on the flight. This will invariably include what elementary skills they will introduce you to, the direction of flight, altitude and a safety brief. With regards to direction of flight, it is not uncommon for the instructor to offer to take you over your home and local area or, if this is too far away, offer to show you a local landmark or a town you may know. Having already made a preliminary visit to the club and seen their aircraft, you should not find the inside of an aircraft too daunting and a shock to the senses. As anticipated, the aircraft will have dual controls, so both you and the instructor can manipulate the control surfaces. You should not need to concern yourself with equipment as a headset will be provided by the club and will be available throughout your training. This will be included in the cost as part of the hourly rate. You should not expect to make any radio calls in your introductory flight, but you will be able to hear all radio communications being made between your aircraft and any radio stations you will be in contact with. You will also be party to other aircraft's transmissions, some of whom will be firing fast-paced dialogue across the airwaves, which may seem intimidating. Take this opportunity to let all communications wash over you, but do not pull up a complete veil of denial and ignorance, as eventually you will be operating the radio. You will be surprised by what procedures and radiotelephony you will pick up just by being exposed to it.

For the purpose of an introductory lesson, the instructor will mainly look to focus on your basic handling skills once established in straight and level flight. In respect of this, do not be deterred by how slick and quick their start-up procedure, checklist completion and radio skills are – their objective is to get you both in the air as swiftly as they are able to, to give you maximum exposure to handling the aircraft. It is unlikely the instructor will allow you to conduct the take-off, though they may ask you to *'follow me through'* with the controls. This will be a familiar phrase throughout the early stages of your training, whereby the instructor will demonstrate a skill or technique and invite you to lightly hold your hands and feet over the controls. The aim of this is to allow you to feel the levels of pressure and deflection of the control inputs they are making. Usually, the first skill introduced by an instructor is maintaining the aircraft in straight and level flight. However, they may also look to introduce a gentle banking turn to the left and right. In essence, the control column is turned toward the desired direction of flight. Once the desired bank angle is achieved, the control column is centralised to cease the continuation of the bank. The aircraft will continue to turn at the set bank angle (with the use of small corrective inputs) until the opposite command is applied to return the aircraft back to straight and level flight. As mentioned, you will be invited to *'follow me through'* once or twice, and soon after, when the instructor is happy that you have grasped the skill, they will hand over the control of the aircraft to you with the announcement *'you have control.'* This is another phrase you will become familiar with inside the cockpit when operating alongside an instructor, examiner or fellow pilot. To this announcement you should reply with the acceptance *'I have control,'* or *'I do not have control'* as the case may be, to avoid any confusion over who is controlling the aircraft. It may seem odd, silly or awkward at first, but this dialogue is a staple part of aviation phraseology. A less-used phrase, but still making the rounds, is *'your aircraft'* and the reply *'my aircraft'*. Besides the obvious milestones in your training, such as going solo, being handed over control of the aircraft for the first time is a very monumental occasion indeed, and one that is often forgotten about (along with the first time you make a radio call).

There will be ample opportunity to take pictures of your surroundings while in flight while command is handed over to your instructor. One of my favourite things about flying is the views and perspective you get from a light aircraft at 2,000 feet. From 2,000 feet, you have enough height and field to see afar, whilst you are still low enough to retain plenty of detail of the world below. This level of perspective you rarely see from an airliner. After all, on take-off a conventional airliner will climb through 2,000 feet within a minute and the detail on the surface quickly disappears into endless rolling fields and small blotches below. Upon landing, it is much the same as you descend through this height on your final approach path. Remember your first flight is supposed to be an enjoyable experience so do not feel that you are at the mercy of the instructor. Besides, for your first flying lesson they are not looking to put you through your paces, their objective is to retain you as a student, so make the most of your first flight by taking some great photos and making some unforgettable memories.

In a similar way to taking off, you are likely to be invited to *'follow me through'* on landing to get a feel for the aircraft and how it responds. To gain the most out of your introductory flight, I would recommend doing this rather than capturing your landing on camera. If in a four-seater aircraft, bring a family member or friend along to record over your shoulder during the landing phase; this footage will be more impressive than your shaky recording out the front and through the propeller. But, more importantly, this will mean you can focus on receiving instruction. There will be plenty of time later in your flight training for a plethora of recording and photo opportunities, so instead focus on the image out the front of the aircraft of the runway approaching. If, and ultimately when, you decide to carry on with your training there will be few opportunities to see the instructor fly the approach down to the runway. Hereafter, they will very quickly begin handing the aircraft over to you more and more in the subsequent lessons; not immediately to land the aircraft but at the very least to bring it down to the threshold.

Upon landing, you may have already made up your mind that flight training is the right course of action for you. In an ideal world, and for the purpose of this book, this would be the best-case scenario. However, it is not uncommon to have mixed or conflicted feelings about your flight experience once it is over. After all, it is likely to be an exhausting, long day and mentally tiring.

As with most things in life, it is easy to take a pessimistic view of the experience and begin mulling over the smaller inconveniences, such as the vibrations mentioned in the previous chapter, rather than the positives that can be taken away. It is important not to amplify these smaller annoyances and allow them to smear what should be an exciting time for you. I recall in my earlier training spending a short period thinking over the positives and negatives of my experience. The overriding pros were naturally the views and the achievement of handling an aircraft – they cannot be equalled. The cons, however, were my initial perspective on the depth and breadth of the content that would need to be learned to fulfil the criteria of the licence, which appeared daunting and intimidating at the time, and the style of instruction, which initially felt almost regimental and military in its delivery.

It must be a part of human nature to focus on the negatives immediately following an event, but what I have found through my experience is that within a few days those negatives fall by the wayside and we tend to remember the better, more positive aspects of an event. Even now, there are times when I fly that I feel frustrated with my performance relating to a particular aspect of the flight. Later, however, those feelings subside, and I remember the experience as a positive one. I think this comes down to another natural human behaviour: our ability to learn from our experiences and adapt our behaviours. I can relate this back to my above 'con' example with regards to the seemingly militaristic and regimental delivery of instruction I was receiving. I took a negative standpoint because this nature and style of tuition was foreign to me. My previous training experiences, such as learning to drive, had always been taught in a more informal, personal style. So I realised, to fulfil my ambition of becoming a pilot, I would need to adapt my expectation and be more flexible in the way I was open to receive tuition. You must be open to this assertive and somewhat direct form of instruction as there is a strong element of discipline required to be a pilot – running through checklists, determining the airworthiness of the aircraft and, ultimately, bearing responsibility for the safe conduct of flight. I personally feel that should you want to become a pilot, you must be able to see past the smaller negatives, such as the ones discussed, and approach training with an open mind, despite issues that may arise and cause you to question your commitment. If you identify with this approach and attitude, then you have the right philosophy to commit and make the decision to continue your training. Not every flight will be positive, but with this attitude you should find you are able to move on and weather any storm that may cause you to falter along the way.

Undertaking training for the PPL is not just a commitment of a financial kind, or one that you dedicate two Saturdays a month to, there is a great deal more learning to further compliment and aid your training that is additional to the minimum 45 flying hours needed to complete the licence. As alluded to in chapter three, there are, of course, nine theoretical ground examinations to pass, as well as the flight radiotelephony operator licence. To pass these elements successfully will require a substantial amount of studying and revision, so be prepared to spend some evenings during your week learning and consolidating your knowledge. These examinations are the minimum requirement for the licence, but you should feel motivated to read further into all aviation topics to give yourself a well-rounded knowledge. This additional work will reflect in your performance during training and may even help you to complete your licence at, or close to, the minimum flight time required. I got the impression from my training club that my eagerness to read into navigation and flight planning helped push my training along. If you are not the sort of person to take the initiative with your further reading and learning, you may find you progress through the syllabus more slowly and will find the club trying to push you along. This will cost you financially through additional lessons, and also in time. So I would advise taking the lead in building your knowledge; this is the kind of commitment that is required and what your training organisation will want to see.

F urther to the minimum flight time and theoretical examination criteria, to hold a Private Pilot's Licence a candidate must also be in possession of a valid medical certificate recognised by EASA. The European regulation that outlines the requirement and criteria for medical certification is the European Commission Regulation no. 1178/2011, which includes, more pertinently, Annex IV – Part-MED, which details the specific medical requirements for the certification of aircrew. This information can be found on the EASA website; however, you will also be able to find this information on your country's aviation authority website.

Technical European Regulation and medical jargon aside, ultimately all you need to know is that you need to gain a Class 2 or Class 1 medical. All the while you are flying with an instructor you are not required to hold a medical, but it will help in progressing your flight training – namely towards your first solo flight – if you are in possession of a valid medical. To that end, I would advise undertaking a medical examination shortly after your first trial lesson, once you have made a commitment to undertaking the training, as you will quickly begin working towards your first solo flight. You do not want your progress hindered by an oversight such as not having a valid medical, as it will delay your solo flight while you await an appointment to see an Aero-Medical Examiner (AME). That is right, no ordinary general practitioner or local surgery can certify you as fit for flight. This falls to a medical examiner educated in the ways of aviation medicine. They may still be a GP but offer the Class 2 medical as an additional service or specialism. Given this niche area of expertise, it is no surprise to find that AMEs are hard to come by, so be prepared to travel some distance to be assessed. A quick internet search will bring up a list of AMEs in your area – but to be extra shrewd, it would be sensible to, again, consult your governing aviation authority. They will have a downloadable list of all certified AMEs in your country, their location/practice and the services they can provide. You should expect to pay in the region of £80-£150 (90-165 €*) for a Class 2 medical, but, of course, this differs from practice to practice and with the service sought.

With regards to the Class 2 and Class 1 medicals mentioned earlier, these are the two medicals that will qualify you for the issue of the PPL. I have written Class 2 first as this is the minimum medical certification standard and the most common medical attained for the issue of the PPL. Upon certification your medical will be valid for 60 months if you are under the age of 40; between 40 and 50 years old a Class 2 medical will be valid for 24 months; and beyond 50 your medical will need to be revalidated every 12 months. In this assessment you should expect to be examined on

---

*   Exchange rate £1 = 1.10 € (Winter 2018)

your medical history, eyesight, hearing and lung function. You may also be expected to provide a urine sample and undergo an electrocardiogram (ECG). That said, however, not all of these assessments will be undertaken by the AME and it will be at their discretion based on the information you provide on your state of fitness. You should usually allow one to two hours for a Class 2 medical examination to be conducted.

A Class 1 medical is the certification required to operate commercially as a professional pilot holding the Airline Transport Pilot Licence (ATPL) or Commercial Pilot Licence (CPL). This examination is a more in depth medical assessment and usually lasts around half a day. There are fewer Aeromedical Centres (AeMCs) than AMEs; however, they are purely specialists in aviation medicine and issuers of Class 1 medicals. Owing to this specialism and the depth of assessment, Class 1 medicals are roughly 3 to 4 times the price of a Class 2 – around £300-£400 (330-440 €*). So why have I chosen to include this? For two reasons: The Class 1, whilst only valid for 12 months (six months if over 60), also includes the Class 2 certification. The second reason is that if you have commercial ambitions for the future, it may be sensible to undergo a Class 1 medical to see if you meet the required medical standards to progress as a commercial pilot. Whilst the Class 1 medical expires within 12 months (long before it would be plausible to gain a commercial licence), you will still hold the Class 2 medical, which is valid for 60 months to cover

---

* Exchange rate £1 = 1.10 € (Winter 2018)

your PPL. Furthermore, you will have an insight into what standard needs to be met to be issued a Class 1 for commercial purposes.

I have undertaken both the Class 2 and Class 1 medical examinations. The Class 1 by and large was the most thorough of the two. My examination was held at the National Air Traffic Service (NATS) Headquarters in Swanwick, Hampshire, which required me to travel three hours from home. I took the initiative to travel the day before and stay nearby to reduce the likelihood of being caught in traffic and being late. Before I attended the assessment I was booked into a local optometrist who checked my prescription and investigated the general health of my eyes. I then reported to the AeMC for a physical assessment that included blood and urine tests, a lung function test and an electrocardiogram. I also completed a detailed questionnaire about my health and behaviours. The assessment in total took around three hours, which is typical for this grade of medical. Regarding the Class 2 medical, this assessment lasted less than 1 hour. I was also fortunate enough to find an AME near where I lived so my medical did not cause too much disruption to my routine. In this appointment, my colour vision was checked along with my visual acuity at close range. Besides this, the assessment was no different to any other general health check I have experienced when visiting my GP.

Whilst the Class 1 medical is not required for the issue of the PPL, it is useful to know and understand the differences, certainly if you have further ambitions with your flying. However, solely for the issue of the PPL, the Class 2 medical is the most appropriate certification to seek out.

A s you progress through the PPL you will inevitably need to invest in some hardware and equipment to help your flight planning, calculation and measurements. There are also other non-aviation specific things that it would be worthwhile investing in too. At multiple stages during your training, there will be a scenario where you will ask your instructor a question and they will reply, 'do you have your air law book?' or 'let me show you on your chart.' So it would be in your best interests to research and invest in this equipment ahead of the time that you need it. Your chosen flying club should have, at the very least, a small inventory of essential items to you get started. I will endeavour to elaborate on a list of items you will need and do so in chronological order.

Once you complete your trial lesson, the club are likely to present you with a certificate commemorating your trial flight. They will inform you that this flight time is valid and can be logged towards completing the minimum 45 hours for the PPL. They are likely to guide you towards purchasing a log book for you to record your hours. Don't fret, this is not a pushy sale or an effort to extort you! If you show the eagerness to continue with your training, you will need somewhere to record your hours so the club should be able to provide you with one. Naturally, they will show you how to fill it in correctly as well. If your plan was always to commit to flying, you could always look to purchase a log book in advance from any reputable online retailer or aviation supply shop. You should look to pay between £10-£20 (11-22 €)* for a log book. The cheaper end of the scale is amply fit for purpose for PPL flying. Should you choose to purchase a log book from the club, you could find the log book is emblazoned with their club logo which may or may not be to your taste. In my youthful naivety, I took the option to purchase a club emblazoned log book which in hindsight I wish I had not. Much like a puppy, a log book is for life not just for Christmas! So whilst I am not too excited about the exterior of my log book (because I did not stay at the club where I undertook my trial lesson), it is an invaluable record of achievement and a possession of mine that is filled with many memories and milestones. Of course, this is purely superficial on my part and your choice is individual.

There may be an option to buy one or more of the Air Pilot Publishing training manuals that form the base of the theory knowledge for the PPL and where the bulk of the theoretical examinations draw their content from. These manuals include Flying Training (1), Air Law & Meteorology (2), Navigation (3), Aeroplane-Technical (4), Human Performances & Operational Procedures (6) and Communications (7). Manual 5 is Radio Navigation & Instrument Flying, which includes more content than what is required for the

---

*   Exchange rate £1 = 1.10 € (Winter 2018)

issue of the PPL; however, it may be good to have it if you have further flying ambitions. I would encourage you to purchase some, if not all, of these manuals from your club in order to support your training organisation. However, on the other hand, if you are not too concerned by the condition of the books you may be able to find some pre-loved copies available online on Amazon or eBay for around £10 each (11 €*). In one instance, I was able to pay a single penny for one of the manuals, so I only had to pay the small delivery charge on top. If you have connections with people who have undertaken flight training you may be in the fortunate position where they could lend or donate you their copies. Some larger online retailers can offer you a saving on a bundle that includes all manuals from 1 through to 7. If you are purchasing new, you should expect to pay in the region of £20 (22 €*) per book or around £120-£140 (132-154 €*) for a bundle. A bundle may also include a mock examination book. These books will become a staple part of your reading and revision.

With regards to basic handling skills, such as climbing and descending, turning etc, there is no checklist per se. Your instructor will teach you the skill and how to execute it proficiently. However, you will need an aircraft-specific checklist for the aircraft you are learning on that covers critical safety and operating procedures. The checklist will include items to look out for on the walk-around procedure and include checks that must be addressed at critical stages of flight, including start-up, pre-take-off, pre-landing etc, as well as emergency and abnormal flight conditions. I would

---

*   Exchange rate £1 = 1.10 € (Winter 2018)

advise purchasing this from the club for no other reason than, whilst you would expect a checklist to be standardised for a single aircraft type, there may be subtle differences in how the club work through and teach their checklists for their aircraft. These will be subtle differences such as the order of checking certain items. For example, your checklist, purchased elsewhere, may direct you to check the transponder towards the end of your after-start checks, whereas your instructor, who will be very fluid and familiar with their own/the club's checklist, may expect to see you check this earlier. It could lead to an awkward back and forth whereby they will highlight that you have missed the item, then you will reply that, 'on my checklist, that item is towards the end,' and then they will suggest you use the club's checklist, and so on and so forth. Long story short, using the checklist that has the club's seal of approval will speed up your checklist procedure and negate any inconsistencies and confusion that could arise, otherwise.

Once you begin taking on more flying responsibilities, such as recording weather information and radio clearances, it would be a good idea to invest in a kneeboard. A kneeboard is a sturdy piece of hardware that provides a surface to write on. They vary in size, but a small folding A5-sized one seems to fit the bill for this kind of flying. Some can be found that include quick reference information, such as the phonetic alphabet and Morse code, already printed on them. Mine has a plastic sheet overlay that allows me to write on it with a semi-permanent pen which I can later erase. The result means less paper and clutter in the cockpit; by now, of course, you will have realised space is at a premium in light aircraft and storage areas are limited or none existent.

Your club may have a second-hand one that they may be able to sell/give to you. A basic kneeboard will set you back £15-£25 (16,5-27,5 €*) if you buy it online.

The following items will be needed in relation to navigation. I briefly alluded to semi-permanent pens above: these are a wise investment as you will be using them a lot in your training when you move onto navigation. If you can, purchase ones with an array of colours, such as black, green, blue and red. These will help you differentiate your markings from the background of your chart. Having different colours can help you categorise the information you are recording. For example, on my chart I would record my groundspeeds in red and my track headings in black so as to not confuse the two. To expand on this, if my route were to see me fly a westerly heading (270 degrees) and I misidentified my groundspeed of 100 as my course to steer I could easily find myself heading in completely the opposite direction. This can then unlock a labyrinth of issues pertaining to becoming lost, being disorientated and managing a massively increased work load that can affect your ability to fly the aircraft effectively. Admittedly, this is an extreme, altogether unlikely, example, but plausible nonetheless.

Which brings me onto the chart – you will need a current, valid and recognised visual flight rules (VFR) chart for the area you are operating in. It is a legal requirement that a VFR chart is carried on board whilst in flight. Also, you cannot operate as a

---

*   Exchange rate £1 = 1.10 € (Winter 2018)

solo pilot unless there is one in the cockpit with you. So, if you are to be sent solo, but still do not have a chart, then you must request the use of your instructor's. The charts used are either the 1:500,000 scale or the lesser-demanded, but more detailed, 1:250,000. The latter being less preferred because of its large scale. Using the larger-scale chart, even over a relatively short flight, may mean you need to unfold the chart, at which point you will understand how un-ergonomic and ill-compatible it is for a light aircraft cockpit.

On an equal par of importance with the VFR chart is the flight computer. It is a computer by name only, as by modern standards it does not resemble a conventional computer. It is, however, a two-sided small handheld wheel and slider. One side is used to provide solutions to wind vector calculations, whilst the reverse is used to calculate answers to basic formulae and simple multiplication and division calculations. It is commonly referred to in aviation as the 'whizwheel' for its ability to spin about its axis. It is a highly accurate instrument for something that appears and reads as being fairly archaic. If you have not seen one before I urge you to, firstly, give it a quick internet search and, lastly, do not be intimidated by its apparent complex appearance. Once studied and understood, it is actually a very simple piece of kit to use. It can be used to calculate drift angle and groundspeed if a wind vector is known. Transversely, if the drift angle and ground speed is known, it can reverse calculate to provide you with the wind vector. Essentially, it is an instrument that can provide you with a value for an unknown variable, should you have other data to input into it to derive an answer.

You do not need to purchase a headset as this will be provided by the club. Even once you have completed the PPL your club will still provide a headset. If you do want to buy one, I would not rush into purchasing a headset until you have researched the wide span of products available as they vary vastly in price and quality – but essentially do the same job. I would suggest seeking the advice of other pilots or your club: their experience should steer you towards a headset that is value for money and fit for purpose.

The items that I have listed above are what I believe to be the bare minimum equipment list to successfully navigate the PPL syllabus. I personally used no more than the above. Of course, there are many additional products, technologies and apps available on the market that are designed to reduce cockpit work load and provide solutions to problems quicker. An example being a crosswind calculator, similar in size to a debit card reader, which you can simply type in the track heading and the wind vector and it will calculate a drift value and wind correction angle to apply to your heading.

Technologies like this are helpful and quick to use in a busy cockpit environment, but they do lend themselves to devaluing the knowledge and mental dexterity of the pilot. All calculations pertinent to flight can be explored on a traditional flight computer. Understanding how to calculate and derive solutions on a flight computer demonstrates better knowledge and airmanship skills. To that end, be cautious about trading off your technical no-how for a speedy solution. If/when technology eventually fails and you have an aircraft technical issue, your raw knowledge, airmanship skills and mental arithmetic will be drawn on – no phone app or quick reference calculator will assist you.

After acquiring all this kit, you will need somewhere to store it all! You will need a flight bag with a decent volume to carry and organise your equipment. These can be picked up relatively cheap online for around £20 (22 €*) at the cheaper end of the spectrum. For this price, you will get a gym-style holdall which should be more than adequate for your needs; no airline pilot trolley case required here!

Before I round off on one of the longer chapters of the book, I really feel it is necessary to discuss second-hand, or pre-loved, products. Learning to fly is quite an expensive undertaking so it will lessen some of the financial pressures if you look at used equipment at this early stage in your flying. After all, brand new equipment can be very expensive; even moderately priced, middle-of-the-market headsets can set you back £400 (440 €*)– the same cost of two to three flying lessons. It is not uncommon to see second-hand items sell for up to 50 per cent less than retail price, and this does not necessarily mean you are buying worn-out, well-used or faulty equipment.

Pilots tend to look after their equipment rather well and sell cheap for a quick sale. All of my rulers, protractors and most of my books were second hand and all were in a very good condition. After

---

*   Exchange rate £1 = 1.10 € (Winter 2018)

all, a book is often only read once (if at all) and a navigation 1:500,000 scale ruler, for the purpose of drawing tracks on charts, is probably only used once or twice a month, so why spend £15 (16,5 €*) on a new one? A good friend of mine purchased a second-hand David Clark H10-13.4 headset for £100 (110 €*) below retail price and they had only been used for 20 flying hours, which is barely anything in the grand scheme of things – a dozen flights, perhaps. Even now, at the time of writing, there are two H10-13.4 headsets available on eBay; the first is buy-it-now for £200 (220 €*) and the second is at auction beginning at £100 (110 €*). I think this is very reasonable when considering these retail new for £340 (375 €*).

---

* Exchange rate £1 = 1.10 € (Winter 2018)

D uring your trial lesson you will have been introduced to the various flight control systems that propel and direct the aircraft. On a basic trainer aircraft, used for the purpose of training students, these control systems are:

Flight Surface Controls

- ✈ The control yoke/stick, which controls the pitch and roll of the aircraft through the deflection of the elevator and ailerons respectively.
- ✈ The rudder pedals, which deflect the rudder on the vertical tailplane. This deflection controls the yaw of the aircraft. This surface provides the same control function as the steering mechanism of a ship.

Engine Controls

- ✈ The throttle, which controls the flow rate of the air/fuel mixture to the engine.

- ✈ The mixture, which allows the pilot to adjust the air/fuel ratio for a more efficient burn at higher altitudes.
- ✈ The carburettor heat control, which delivers engine heat to the throat of the carburettor to clear any ice that may exist. This depends on the aircraft type, as fuel-injector aircraft do not require a carburettor.

The latter two engine controls may have been briefly referred to, but not described in depth, as for the purpose of a trial lesson their effects do not demonstrate a visual or tangible consequence that, say, increasing the throttle or banking the aircraft would produce.

After this brief introduction to the aircraft controls, it would be representative of your commitment to succeed if you were then able to go away and read about these controls systems further. Drawing from personal experience, I left my introductory lesson without using the rudder pedals or understanding their purpose. In my mind, directional control was the work of the ailerons and elevator: if I wanted to aim at a point below and to the left of me I would bank towards it with the ailerons and aim down towards it using the elevator. This led me to ask, '*why the need for the rudder pedals and what purpose did they serve if I could achieve all direction using one control – the yoke?*' Quite simply, the answer lies within the Air Pilot's Flying Manual (no answers given away here). However, for my own style of learning I also asked the instructor to impart on me their interpretation of the explanation, which ultimately made things click.

By the end of your PPL, you will have a concise understanding of how the aircraft operates. It is demonstrative of a good pilot to understand what mechanical responses are as a result of their inputs. Unlike jet-liners that employ sophisticated fly-by-wire or hydraulic systems, the humble light aircraft's control surfaces are deflected by a series of hinge lines and pulleys. Familiarise yourself with how they work and interact. Most light aircraft elevator and aileron mechanical lines, whilst controlled by the same input, the control yoke, are independent of one another. This further reading is important for your development as a pilot, as knowing these behind-the-scenes systems, even at a glance, will assist you when troubleshooting if you experience the unenviable situation of control surface loss or difficulties.

With regards to engine control, *The Air Pilot's Manual 4: The Aeroplane – Technical* will cover all engine-related topics such as engine operations and limitations and how, as a pilot, you can monitor and run the engine safely. If you have experience of working with or on engines, or have an interest in mechanics, then wrapping your head around this topic should not be too taxing. If, however, you are not well versed in the ways of the internal combustion engine and self-contained magneto systems, then the aforementioned book will give a pilot-level insight. Furthermore, there are some very clear and well-presented videos on YouTube covering this intimidating and, seemingly, rough-around-the-edges topic. The technical aspects of flying can put off prospective students; largely those who just want to fly and have no interest in what makes a machine fly. I once fell into that category as I had no interest in the physics and mechanics of flight. As someone whose mechanical and technical ability bore no success other than replacing a bicycle chain in 2008, I distanced myself from this subject matter for as long as I could. In hindsight, however, I can see how this delayed my progression through the theoretical examinations.

Ultimately, the PPL is designed for anyone who is interested, physically fit and of sound mind to pass. To that end, the content is not that deep and demanding. Once I tackled the technical arena of the theory I was surprised by how manageable it was. Any independent reading regarding this topic, at the early stages or later in the PPL, will serve you well.

Your club and instructor will be very impressed by any additional reading. Discussing and talking through what you have learned with your instructor will serve to aid their understanding of your knowledge and ability. It will also provide an opportunity for them to give you feedback and any additional or corrective information. Instructor aside, there are also other outlets where one can seek clarification. That is one of the great things about flying – the knowledge is readily available in books, from peers or online. I know of no other community where there is such free and readily available information to help learning –so long as you are prepared to seek it out. A word of caution, however, whilst the community is rich with contemporaries who are willing to share information and knowledge, I would strongly advise, as before, running anything you have learned, or been told, past your instructor, and never accept or rely on any knowledge imparted on you if you do not understand it 100 per cent.

W hile airborne, a pilot needs a constant stream of data available to them in order to manage and maintain a safe and orderly flight. The aircraft's instruments and management systems provide this information. The primary flight instruments display the aircraft's flight condition in an easily interpreted representation. A basic trainer aircraft will include the following six flight instruments:

- ✈ The attitude indicator, which conveys the aircraft's pitch and bank angles relative to the horizon.
- ✈ The airspeed indicator, which displays the speed of the aircraft through the air mass it is travelling.
- ✈ The altimeter, which is configurable to produce a height or altitude above ground level or above mean sea level, respectively, with reference to barometric atmospheric pressure.
- ✈ The heading indicator, which provides the pilot with directional informational.

These four instruments are fundamental in navigation as they provide information on height, speed, direction and orientation. There are two further instruments considered as of primary importance, and they are:

- ✈ The turn and slip indicator, which informs the rate of turn and the balance of the aircraft in a turn, or lack thereof, known as slip or skid.
- ✈ The vertical speed indicator, which displays the rate of change of altitude in feet or metres per minute.

Whilst on first inspection the inside of a cockpit can seem to be a labyrinth of instruments and dials, once you have an understanding of the purpose and function of each one, the instrument panel becomes a less intimidating beast. By the time you become proficient with the fundamental flying skills, such as climbing, descending and turning, you will be equally familiar with these instruments and how they display the behaviours of flight for you to interpret. This skill to read the instruments will come naturally and you will be surprised by how little conscious effort is required to read the data displayed. Of course, these instruments have been developed, tweaked and ergonomically designed to have a user-friendly interface.

With the advent of GPS tracking, one could be forgiven for thinking that data pertaining direction, speed and height (both altitude and vertical speed) is provided by satellite tracking. However, this is not the case, not even for the most modern commercial airliners. The aircraft themselves have an array of sensors that collate this information and relay it to the cockpit. In more advanced airliners, this information is transmitted electronically by wire and is reinterpreted on LCD screens. On more dated aircraft, or those that you are likely to train on, these sensors are highly sensitive instruments that transmit the data mechanically through a series of cogs and cranks and display it visually on dials and gauges through pointers.

For the purpose of understanding light aircraft that you are likely to train on, I would suggest researching and reading up on gyroscope and pitot-static systems. The instruments highlighted at the beginning of this chapter draw their data from these types of systems. A full breakdown of flight instrumentation and where and how they collect data is covered in *The Air Pilot's Manual 4: The Aeroplane – Technical*. Having a working knowledge of these aircraft systems will aid you in flight if you experience some technical difficulties. For example, if your attitude indicator does not produce a true reflection of your actual bank and pitch angle, or your heading indicator becomes unreliable and does not match your magnetic compass, you should be able to determine that you have an inoperable gyroscope – potentially to do with suction. In this case, you should check your suction gauge, which should indicate whether or not the suction is operating within limits. Again, refer to your training manual and seek the expertise of an instructor to clarify this information.

I f you have had no experience of flying in light aircraft other than your flight training, then give some time and thought to what flying will be like post-training. During your training, you learn to become a *pilot under tuition*, following direction and instruction. That said, the syllabus is designed in such a way that as a student you ought to become more autonomous as you transition through the programme, from student to pilot-in-command; through flight-planning and solo flying elements. In the earlier stages of training, however, it may be difficult to envisage what the end product will be like. With a few hours under your belt, now would be a great time to fly as a passenger and observe a qualified private pilot. Even if you have had previous experience in a light aircraft as a passenger prior to commencing your training, it would be beneficial to see this again now you are equipped with a better understanding of operating an aircraft.

Hopefully, at this point in your interaction with the club and its members you would have met other students who are further along the process, and qualified pilots who are prepared to share advice and tips, with the latter, perhaps, even offering to take you flying some time. If you already know someone who is a qualified pilot then great, but, if not, definitely take up the opportunity to fly with a qualified club member. This insight into post-training flying will give you something to focus on and work towards. While learning to fly, the cockpit atmosphere is more tense as you learn new skills and refine techniques; so flying with a qualified pilot, on the other hand, will provide an insight into how much the workload and stress levels lessen with increased proficiency once qualified. It is refreshing to witness procedures that you experience as being demanding in your status as a student executed smoothly by a qualified pilot. If you fly with a club member, it will also give you an insight into the standard that the club expect you to operate to before they sign you off as competent and able to fly club aircraft once qualified. Even with the PPL in their possession, it is likely that the club member will still be receiving periodic instruction and check-rides from the club's instructors to maintain their skills.

When I was around the 15-hour mark, I was curious to see another aircraft, pilot and area without necessarily paying a training rate for instruction at an unfamiliar club. There was a free-of-charge option to fly with a club member as a passenger, but this would have seen me fly from the same airfield and around the same area. I found an alternative option by seeking out an online cost-sharing platform that offers the public (me, in this case) a cheap flight experience option, which, in turn, subsidises the pilot's operating costs. EASA rules stipulate that a pilot may not operate and execute the privileges of a PPL for commercial or revenue generating purposes. However, EASA allows for the cost of operating a flight to be divided amongst the operator and their passengers (up to a maximum of six passengers). The EU regulation that enshrines this stipulation is EU no 965/2012. This legislation also allows a pilot to advertise their trips as any monies received do not go towards personal or commercial financial gain but instead spread the burden of direct costs – these costs include landing fees, fuel and other on-the-day operating incursions. Cost-sharing platforms tend to target the area of the market interested in flight experiences and once-in-a-lifetime experiences. These platforms offer the consumer around a 50 per cent saving on what they would otherwise spend at a traditional club. I paid £80 (88 €*) for an hour's flight with a qualified pilot – presumably they paid the remaining £80 or so, and the online platform takes a cut. A flying club would charge anywhere between £150-£200 (165-220 €*) for the same kind of experience. The gulf in price is largely owed to the need for a flying club to pay wages and make a profit. These variables are not factors in cost-sharing. With that in mind, some flying clubs do not authorise their club members to operate these cost-sharing flights on club aircraft. From a club's perspective there are concerns regarding competition and liability in the event of an accident. Get involved in the discussion around cost-sharing with your club, fellow members or any pilots you meet – it is a very current and topical subject in aviation at the moment and it produces a varied spread of interesting opinions and viewpoints.

In advance of my cost-sharing flight experience, I made contact with the pilot and let them know that I was undertaking flight

---

*   Exchange rate £1 = 1.10 € (Winter 2018)

training and explained what I wanted to take away from the experience. The flight time could not be logged as the pilot was not an instructor and this was not to be a commercial flight. Any 'hands-on' experience was a bonus in my opinion, and I managed my expectation accordingly. My plan was to observe their checklist and radio procedure and understand their decision-making processes. It also gave me the opportunity to observe a flight from the right-hand seat, which is not a commonly available opportunity when flying with an instructor. Having a common interest in aviation made the flight very enjoyable, and I had the opportunity to overfly some familiar territory from some several years previous when I studied in Southampton. This also helped me to realise some flying objectives and goals I sought to achieve once qualified. I decided off the back of this scenic observation flight that my first land away sortie would see me return back to this area, but, of course, as pilot-in-command to visit some of the old haunts I used to frequent as a fresh-faced teenager.

Personal niceties aside, I took away a lot in terms of what standards and expectations I should demand of myself. I was pleasantly surprised to hear the pilot ask for my input and advice on varying stages of flight and ask how his handling of the aircraft differed to how I was being taught. This alone was quite empowering as up to this stage I felt very much like a novice and unable to offer anything to an experienced and qualified pilot. Also, this flight gave me the opportunity to experience another aircraft for the first time – a PA28. In chapter five I touched upon how I felt it was inappropriate for a club to move a student between aircraft types to suit their schedule if they are overbooked or short of aircraft.

I still believe this to be true whilst under instruction; however, for the purpose of observing and seeing what lies beyond the PPL training syllabus, flying on a different type will give you a greater appreciation. After all, learning to fly in a Cessna 152 does not mean you are committed, ball and chain, to that aircraft for evermore. I was exposed to the differences in handling, power and operational procedures of the type. I recall in particular my concern when the pilot suggested around 20 minutes into our flight that we ought to fly around the coastline of the Isle of Wight; an endeavour that in a Cessna 152 would take around 40 minutes. Of course, this was no cause for fret, as the PA28 completed this circumnavigation in 30 minutes, allowing plenty of time to return to the airfield. Despite flying at 2,000 feet, I was still able to sense the increased speed over the steadier Cessna 152, a skill that I was not aware I had in my arsenal. It was from this point onwards I began to pay attention to our aircraft's rate of progress over the ground and how it varied depending whether we were flying with the wind or against it.

You may find in the earlier stages of training that your handling is all over the place as you focus your energies on maintaining your heading, altitude and passing messages over the radio. In amongst this workload, you may find it difficult to 'feel' the aircraft. Every now and then it pays dividends to handover control to somebody else. When flying as a passenger with another pilot operating, and therefore not manoeuvring the aircraft yourself, you are able to spend more time observing the aircraft and its behaviours. This provides you with the opportunity to identify and assess how differently you would handle the aircraft, if any different at all. As you progress through the syllabus, there will be times when your instructor hands the aircraft over to you, and when they say *'you have control'*, without much directed or conscious thought, you will reconfigure the aircraft into what feels right for you.

A ssuming you are now around the five to 10-hour mark, you should have been fully exposed to the checklist procedure of the aircraft you are training on. As you transition from external checks to start up, to take-off etc, your loyal and reliable checklist should be close to hand and frequently referenced. Quite likely, you are still being prompted by your instructor a great deal of the time – either for missing an item or the checklist all together! Try not to let this wear you down. Given that the PPL syllabus is a 45-hour course, you may falsely assess that by the five to 10-hour mark (around 15-20 per cent of the total duration) you should be at the stage where you are demonstrating some fluency and speed with the checklist. This should not be the case and you should not expect this of yourself. An aircraft checklist is quite a lengthy and menacing document to read – it would take some demonstration of character and dedication to commit it all to memory. But there is no need to be that person. Actually, you may be surprised to discover that most instructors would not recommend you do this in case you miss an item that is critical to the safe conduct of flight. There are checks that may become routine through practice, but be forgiving of yourself, and feel no shame in taking your time going through your checklist. After all, flying an aircraft is not something you do daily (at least not at this stage), and there are often long periods in between flights where your ability to recount may become fogged. Besides, it demonstrates good airmanship to be accurate and thorough with your checks.

Ironically, it was the longest part of the checklist that I found to be the easiest to remember and execute, purely because of its logical process – and that was the external walk around. By the end of my training my walk-around technique was refined to a streamlined procedure. To pan around and check the aircraft in a logical clockwise motion from a starting point made logical sense to me. I found that my external checks, which had about 50 lines, were actually a very fluid process. Once I had checked an item, I found that constantly pausing to read the next line (and repeating this so on and so forth) really fractured my checklist procedure and by the time I got to, say, the fifth item, what I had checked before had been forgotten. It would be of good airmanship to practice your walk-around checks even if you are not flying. Your club should be welcoming of you to go out to the aircraft while on the ground and run mock checks and drills. Whilst also having your checklist to hand for reference, I would recommend practising the walk around without relying on the checklist. Then go back and cross check what items you missed. This should not be seen as an exercise to make your checklist redundant but as a means to streamline your external walk around.

There will also be things on the checklist that you may not be confident about. For example, it is all well and good pulling your carburettor heat to 'hot', but what are you *actually* checking? Anyone can follow a checklist, but it is a sign of a good pilot if they know the intricacies behind what they are checking. Another key thing when running your checklists is are you actually checking the item? I was constantly being scorned for reading my checklist and pointing to the item rather than doing my checks on them. An example of this being when 'checking' my ammeter to confirm it was charging – the ammeter being the instrument that measures the current in the aircraft's circuit –I used to just point at it and read 'ammeter – charging' from the script in my hand, without really checking or knowing what I was looking for. It was only when my instructor stopped me and asked 'what are you actually looking for?' did I come to realise I did not actually know. The ammeter display has a needle pointer on a scale from (usually) -60 amps to +60 amps and the needle largely *appears* to sit on zero; central to the scale. So, why was I happy to announce it was charging when on inspection it appeared to read zero all the time? Two reasons. The first was that every time I had previously checked the ammeter it had produced the same value and nothing had gone wrong, technically speaking, up to that point. And secondly, and more worryingly, I did not really understand what it, or I, was doing. I was challenged on why I was agreeing it was charging (a positive value) when the pointer suggested a zero value. I apologised and explained my above reasons and ignorance. As it happened, the aircraft was not defective and the values were within limits. It just so happened that the aircraft type I trained on would produce a value that was ever-so-slightly in the positive reason. Overall, the ammeter debacle was a learning experience that highlighted the need to understand what and why you are checking items.

The main point to take away from this chapter is not the need to remember your checklist like a well-practised speech or catchy lyric, but instead to highlight the need for you to take your time, always reference your checklist and really understand what it is you are checking.

O ne of the main sticking points throughout training for the PPL is the radio and radiotelephony procedure. Learning how to operate and communicate on the radio is a recurring feature in discussions regarding the difficulties in gaining a PPL. The most common anxieties relate to keeping up with the radio chit-chat, confidence in transmitting and learning how to operate the radio.

Depending on where you learn to fly, your exposure to radio procedure will vary greatly. The term air traffic control is used as an umbrella term and has become synonymous with aviation radiotelephony; however, it is only one of three kinds of radio service that an airfield can provide. The other two services are flight information service and air-to-ground service. Only an air traffic control officer can provide you with instructions and clearances – phrases such as 'cleared to land' that we are familiar with. A flight information service officer can provide you with taxi instructions but cannot issue clearances for take-off and landing but will instead guide you to take these actions at your discretion. The air-to-ground radio operator is only qualified to provide you with information such as barometric pressure for the altimeter setting and the runway in use and circuit pattern; all other decisions regarding the manoeuvring of the aircraft are determined by the pilot at their sole discretion. Flight information services and air-to-ground services are usually found at smaller or unlicensed airfields, respectively. On the topic of licensed or non-licensed; to be a licenced aerodrome, the airfield must conform to standards relating to taxiway and runway dimensions, signs, lighting and emergency facilities as stipulated by the relevant national aviation authority.

Confidence using the radio will only arrive and develop by being hands on with the radio. To that end, I would advise taking any opportunity to make calls when prompted by your instructor. In a well-planned and executed flight, with no unexpected disturbances, the radio calls you should expect to make will be fairly uniform and almost procedural. Your radio workload is at its maximum when flying in the circuit; you are receiving and reading back clearances (if at a controlled airfield), reporting positions and looking out for, and acknowledging, traffic reports. You are expected to manage this verbal workload whilst also handling the aircraft. It is at this stage when you are likely to be invited to take more control of the radio communications.

One may see it as a baptism of fire but there is a reason for being thrown in at the deep end like this: it is to develop the ability to manage multiple tasks at once. It may seem like a difficult undertaking to manage both flying and communicating at the same time. Whilst this is true, it is best to learn early on. It will be a demonstration of your eagerness and will to succeed that you attempt to grasp the radio even if you do feel a bit silly or unsure of what calls you are making. Always remember that you will have an instructor next to you on hand to assist with the radio should you struggle with a call or reply. There is no shame or embarrassment in making a wrong call or repeating back a wrong clearance. We all have to learn at some stage and, contrary to popular belief, air traffic control is there to assist you, not to catch you out! You will be given more credit for trying than being scorned for making an error. Be welcoming to criticisms and feedback on, and about, your radio etiquette by your instructor – their comments are not designed to be an assault on your character but a means to correct and direct you. Occasionally, you will make a blunder or forget the required etiquette. Forgive yourself and move on. There were countless times early on in my training where I broke etiquette and became overly familiar or colloquial. These kind of mistakes are natural and can be allowed for, after all, it is not every day you are injected into such an environment. Even now, I overhear pilots on the radio occasionally break etiquette, become flustered or forget their phraseology. It happens, and we must learn to embrace it. All I can advise is that you try to remain calm and plan what you are going to say before transmitting. You will be surprised how many pilots do not follow this simple process. If you are overworked or need to focus your energy on flying the aircraft then communication with air traffic control does not have to be your priority and they will understand this. Remember the mantra: aviate, navigate and communicate – in that order. If you do have the time, you are within your remit to make the radio call 'standby, *your call sign*' to buy you some time.

It is likely that your club will provide you with a basic radio call sheet that will guide you through, logically, the calls you will be expected to make. If not, there are endless open resources available online that can act as a prompt sheet or manual for radiotelephony procedure. However, do be wary! Some videos you may stumble across on YouTube may appear on face value to have some slick and fast radio chat going on. However, with a keen ear you may spot their radio conduct is sloppy and not up to the levels of proficiency required – check in the comment section on flying videos you watch for other pilot's feedback, both constructive and critical. They may offer some good feedback and points that you may not have picked up on. A further warning! Whilst comments in videos may offer an opinion, remember their words are only that: an opinion. I can tell you now, the majority of people commenting on these videos are not themselves qualified or in a position to pass judgement. For any feedback on radiotelephony, consult your instructor.

A sensible document to consult when tackling the radio is *The Air Pilot's Manual 7: Communications*. If you are UK-based student, you can also consult the *Radiotelephony Manual –CAP413*, which seeks to provide pilots and air traffic service personnel with a guide to the clear and standard phraseology used in the UK. If you are Europe-based student whose training falls under the EASA jurisdiction you may look to consult the *EGAST Radiotelephony Guide for VFR Pilots* available from the EASA website. The governing body for international aviation that sets compliance and safety standards, the International Civil Aviation Organization (ICAO), also has its own universal publication from which all other subsequent authorities produce their procedures. This document is called *The Manual of Radiotelephony Doc 943*. These manuals provide a guide and instruction on how to make correct, concise and clear radio calls during all stages of flight, including emergency and distress scenarios. Impress your instructor by letting them know you are aware of, and have consulted, these documents. As I have mentioned in previous chapters, you will get through the PPL quicker and at, or near, the minimum hours if you show your commitment and eagerness. Finding your proficiency on the radio is a big step towards achieving this. You do not need to be a master of the radio, just proficient enough to communicate effectively.

F urther to the checklist and radio, through your flight training you will be introduced to an entire new vocabulary and phraseology. Many words referenced in aviation draw parallels with and are influenced by the maritime sector. During the period that powered flight was first achieved, ships were the peak of engineering. Not only did ships represent the advances in engineering, they also represented the countries whose flags they flew under. Battleships, in particular, represented strength. As such, a country's naval fleet became a symbol of their power and influence on the world stage. With the advent of powered flight, many terms associated with navigation and shipping were simply adopted into the newly formed aviation terminology.

To avoid any embarrassing faux-pas or slip-ups, it is best to brief yourself on the correct terminologies. Inevitably, you will pick them up as you progress through, but I would advise getting ahead of the game. In relation to your radio procedure, you will deliver a better account of yourself if you can refer and communicate using the correct terms. For example, if there is an aircraft in close proximity to you and you have made visual contact, rather than saying to air traffic control that the aircraft is to your right, you should instead report they are to your starboard position. Or, perhaps, even give their relative direction in relation to the 12-hour clock positions. In this example, the aircraft would be at your nine o'clock position. Minor slip-ups in a more informal environment can be forgiven. That said, no one is likely to correct you over the radio if you do make a mistake, besides your instructor. However, it is in the interest of the wider community that your radio procedure is proper.

In aviation, there are thousands of acronyms. Thankfully, not all of them need to be known for the purpose of the PPL. Some of them are everyday phrases we use, such as ETA, which we all know to represent estimated time of arrival, and PPL itself! However, there are many that are aircraft and aviation related that you will not come across elsewhere. You will not be tested on them per se, but having an understanding of the basic abbreviations and acronyms will be a good indicator to your instructor that you are putting the work in. If your instructor is referring to something using an acronym and you are not sure what it represents, always ask in order to seek clarification. In one particular lesson, while I was undergoing training in the circuit, my instructor indicated that we were going to cover an RTO in our next lesson. I had no idea what they meant until they explained the procedure, then I realised they were referring to a rejected take off.

ICAO has compiled a comprehensive list of abbreviations and acronyms, and their respective decodes. It is called *Abbreviations and Codes Doc 8400*. This document can be found online. A good tip is to take notes of various acronyms and abbreviations as and when you see them. Later, check them against the aforementioned document. Being a pilot is a continuous learning experience and you will find you will continue to pick up on these further '–isms'. Even as recent as my latest flight I learned there was three-letter acronym for aerodrome chart – ADC.

Further to a list of acronyms, ICAO has produced a document detailing standardised units of measurement to be used –*Annex 5 – Units of Measurements to be Used in Air and Ground Operations*. This document includes a vast list of many forces and velocities and how, as pilots, we quantify them. Included, of course, are the more humbling units that you will be familiar with through your training, such as quantifying speed in knots; recording altitude in feet; and transmitting on frequencies using Hertz. Whilst through practice and repetition you will become familiar with the correct terms, it is useful to know where to locate this information. Surprisingly, there are still many pilots who make minor errors in their reports. For example, we measure visibility in metres or kilometres. However, you can be sure you will overhear a pilot on frequency relay a reported visual range in miles.

In terms of the aircraft itself, you will find many items that may appear comparable to a car, but instead have completely different names. The main 'gotcha' is the yoke, often mistermed as a steering wheel. Another is gear being miscalled the wheels. You could search the internet for diagrams to better verse yourself with aircraft components. Though, unlike abbreviations and terminologies, I am sure learning these terms will be comparatively easier, and probably achieved through exposure during your lessons.

As a natural lead on from the reassurances of using the radio, it is important to pause and reflect on the achievements you will have made up to this point. With a solo flight on the horizon, it is likely that there have been more successes than you are probably giving yourself credit for. It is human nature for us to reflect on, and mull over, the negatives. This is probably because we take more away emotionally from the negatives, and also because we use the negatives as an opportunity to better ourselves. If you are able to take the setbacks and mistakes on board as a learning point and address them then you are on the right track to success. A great piece of advice given to me by one of my instructors was that:

'If you have the ability to identify where, and when, you are going wrong, you also have the ability to fix it.'

And those words, in my opinion, are a good place to start from when we have those moments of self-doubt.

was fortunate enough to train at a flying school where I was able to meet other members and pilots quite easily. Quite often I would arrive early for my flying lesson and stay for several hours after to talk with other students, instructors and characters passing through about all things flying. This was natural owing to the way the club was run, and this kind of interaction was actively encouraged. This social element, in my opinion, was one of the unique selling points of the school I trained at. On the other hand, I have visited other flying organisations where a social atmosphere does not exist and they function more like a business than a club. In these environments students arrive 30 minutes before their flight, brief, fly, pay then leave. This tends to happen at clubs that have large fleets and multiple instructors to co-ordinate and manage. Though not exclusively, the club environment, in these instances, becomes too busy to facilitate conversation and, in turn, the atmosphere deters students and members from engaging. I was so used to a casual and approachable atmosphere during my training that when I moved my flying elsewhere I was, at first, shocked to find my presence was processed much like what I would experience at the dentist. That is not to say the club is not an effective training school - but it is important to have a good level of exposure to the social and networking side of things. After all, you do not want to gain your PPL and not know anyone else qualified who you can fly with.

Any good club is likely to hold social events throughout the year, ranging from summer BBQs, dinner and dance evenings, wings presentations and meals out. Potentially, the cost of tickets or attendance to these events can be subsidised through holding a club membership. Typically, if the club holds a BBQ they will request that members bring some food and drink. These social events are a must if you have been struggling to meet people on days when you have been at the club. Not only will you be able to meet other club members at these events, it is likely you will meet pilots from other airfields, clubs and organisations. You will be surprised by the range of contacts you can meet at these types of functions. Through attending a single dinner and dance evening, I was able to meet several experienced airline pilots and trainers, an air traffic controller and a pilot union leader, to name a few. I was pleasantly surprised by the diversity and experience in attendance, all of whom were eager to connect and exchange contact numbers and emails etc. Do not pass up the opportunity to attend these kinds of events, they are invaluable occasions to network and you never know what opportunity may arise as a result.

If you are tech and social media savvy then looking to create and develop an online network may be an option for you. There are opportunities to *meet* other students who are going through a similar journey and who may be able share their journey, thoughts and insights. I would strongly recommend becoming involved in the online community. Largely, and more frustratingly, because airfields and clubs are scarce and not as physically frequent as leisure centres, dance clubs or any other hobbying community, for example. Furthermore, even if you are fortunate to live near your club you cannot be sure other members do as well. I had to travel a modest 26 miles to my club when I lived in the southeast of England. Another club member, who became a good friend in the community, had to travel 40 miles in the opposite direction. That 66-mile gulf made socialising and keeping in contact difficult for us both.

Once qualified, your flying will take you geographically to different places, so having a network of contacts around the country or area you fly will enrich your experience. Putting in some effort to make contacts now will certainly pay off once you have your prized PPL. Using online social media platforms, I was able to make contact with pilots at six different airfields around the UK before I had even completed my skills test. To eventually fly in and meet these contacts for lunch or a coffee, or to even go flying with them, was a motivator in getting me through the licence. Also, you will find having contacts at different airfields will assist you greatly in your flight planning and navigation. One of the contacts I mentioned earlier was based at Stapleford in Essex, UK. In anticipation of my upcoming navigation exercise to Southend (a mere 30 miles from Stapleford), I made contact and asked if they had ever been to Southend before, given their close proximity. Not surprisingly, they had been, and as a result I was offered a huge amount of information ranging from the arrival and departure procedure to where I could find a toilet to use! Whilst all navigational and flying data, such as aerodrome charts, can be retrieved from your governing aviation authority's Aeronautical Information Service (AIS – more of that later), nothing comes close to real experience, especially because you can ask questions and seek clarification on points that are not covered in the AIS. These are things that only come with experience, such as 'as you taxi around the corner of C1 stick to the centreline and not off onto the disused taxiway like I did.' Advice like this really helps.

The use of social media such as Instagram and Facebook can bring real positives to your training and flying as a whole – so long as you are using it for the right reasons and it remains fit for purpose, as you originally intended it. I joined Instagram to network and meet other enthusiasts and I can confidently say I achieved the goal I set myself. The aviation community on Instagram is incredibly positive and reassuring, and I was pleasantly surprised by how much encouragement from others and self-motivation can be found on that particular platform. I have been able to share some amazing photos, some of which are included in this publication. The feedback has been wholly upbeat and I too have been able to leave some positive comments on some truly meaningful and great content shared by other users. Try not to be discouraged by other users who abuse Instagram for their own superficial gain. These social media platforms have the ability to instil feelings of inadequacy and anxiety; a result of comparing one's life with another's whose appears more rewarding and/or fulfilling... so long as you remain true to your objectives and what you want to gain from social media then that is something to draw success from. It's a melancholic disclaimer but something that I feel needs highlighting in our modern, social media age.

With a flying club presence, social events and a developing wider network in aviation, you will find that by the time you complete the PPL you will have ample social and flying opportunities available to get you introduced and started in recreational flying post-training. The first people I turned to once I completed my licence were the contacts I had made at the club and those I had met online, both of whom helped me in the transition from student to qualified pilot. You run the risk of falling out of love with flying if you have no motivators or people to share your passion with once you gain your licence, so ensure along the way you make some good contacts.

A great way to integrate more seamlessly into the club is to offer to help out around the club with the various day-to-day tasks. A flying club is often a busy environment and your help, in whatever scale, is likely to be most appreciated. This is especially the case if the flying school you train at is a small organisation, with minimal staffing levels.

Particularly in the gliding community, helping out with the running of the operation and schedule is an integral function of being a member. Members must be on hand all day and willing to take part in ground duties when not flying, such as preparing and launching other glider pilots. This is not an expectation when training as a private pilot, but there may be times when your help is requested, and as an eager student you should demonstrate a willingness to help. Typically, as a student you will book a one-and-a-half or a two-hour slot to cover a one-hour flight. However, be prepared to stay around a little longer as, invariably, the flying itinerary can, and more than likely will, fall behind schedule. If you arrive in good time for your two-hour slot, you may find you are still at the club for at least four to five hours. Rather than sitting around idle, it would be in your best interests to get involved. There is always something to be getting on with, whether it is scanning documents or making a round of tea. On occasions, you may be needed to man the desk to greet new students or flight experience customers while the club co-ordinator tends to various tasks about the airfield. Having this responsibility will go a long way to making you feel involved in the club. Remember that as a member you are also an ambassador for the club.

As a student, there is great value in being active in the club environment on a busy flying day as there are elements of airmanship you would otherwise not experience if you were not. Allow me to elaborate on this point. When you walk out to the aircraft at the beginning of your lesson to do your walk around (by the way, how is that coming along?), do you give much thought to who positioned the aircraft there, how it was fuelled and by whom? Was the aircraft tied down before you got there? In the earlier stages of training you may not have asked these questions as you were mainly focussed on flying the aircraft, but as you spend more time around the aircraft you will eventually develop a curiosity about how it is stored and maintained. One of the first tasks of the morning at a flying club is assigning the aircraft and instructors to slots in order to work out which aircraft need preparing for the day's flying. Dependent on the airfield and/or hangarage arrangements, the required aircraft will then need to be towed into position. If an aircraft is parked outside overnight, there may be a need to untie the aircraft from its securing. These are all tasks that you as a club member can be and, as I believe, should be involved in. I feel those students who progress through the PPL without tying down or uncovering an aircraft, or who have never refuelled an aircraft are at a disadvantage in the 'real world' once their licence is issued.

The club manager at the school I trained at was a fantastic and attentive lady. Always mindful not to inconvenience any of her students, she would strive to ensure all the aircraft were ready and prepared: untied, uncovered, refuelled and water checks complete by the time her first students arrived. This fore work helped the flying schedule get off to a good start! However, she was quite surprised, and equally reassured, when I and few other students said we were quite keen to help out with these tasks and learn these important airmanship skills. By doing so, the morning checks and duties were completed in good time and we were all able to take something away from the experience. Having this level of commitment to your training helps the development of trust. Your club can witness, first hand, your enthusiasm and, coupled with you advancing in your training, they are further exposed to your development as a pilot. This further aids your case as you approach more critical stages in your training, such as your first solo flight and cross-country navigation exercises.

In summary, there are multiple benefits to take away from assisting and lending a hand at the club. Not least, you give a good account of yourself, widen your contacts, build relationships and trust and pick up rudimental airmanship skills – skills that are not necessarily covered as part of the syllabus. The reason is perhaps to see if you, as the student, will seek them out.

Other knowledge I feel is important to have but is not necessarily imparted to you is the inner workings of the engine and what lies beneath the cowlings. You will inevitably be tested on technical elements of PPL flying through two theoretical exams: The Aircraft General Knowledge and Principles of Flight. I would guide you towards *The Air Pilot's Manual 4: The Aeroplane – Technical* book for the intricacies and depth of knowledge you will be required to learn. However, besides studying for the theoretical exams, there is no real exposure to the engine other than through diagrams in the aforementioned manual. Having conducted a few solo walk arounds and pre-flight checks, you will have checked the engine oil and likely conducted a fuel drain to check for water contamination.

Unfortunately, to get a closer look at the mechanisms beneath the engine cowling you are likely to need the supervision of an aircraft engineer or an experienced club member. If your club is large enough it may have its own Part 145 (or equivalent if non-EASA) maintenance accreditation. With this approval certificate, your club will be able to maintain their own aircraft. If your club is a smaller entity they may have their aircraft serviced elsewhere by a third-party contractor. For these smaller clubs they may have their third-party maintenance conducted at the same airfield by a maintenance provider based there for convenience reasons or through existing relationships. Relationships and networking will be recurring themes throughout your training and subsequent flying. If you require advice or help but do not know someone directly, rest assured you will know someone mutually who can put you in touch. To that end, if your club does not have its own maintenance facility but does acquire the services of a maintenance provider at the airfield, they may be able to organise a visit for you or escort you over to the aircraft.

If your club has its own maintenance facility then enquire about organising a visit to see an aircraft undergoing work or servicing. If you are a frequent visitor to the club you may have already been introduced to the aircraft mechanics and engineers – as mentioned before; this is where networking and attending social events and offering to help out pays off.

Organising such a visit should not cause too much of an inconvenience and is likely to be warmly welcomed, not only by the club but also by the engineers. In a similar display that is evident between the different branches of the armed forces, there is a friendly rivalry between pilots and engineers. They are two mutually respectable disciplines that work in unison to fulfil the club's operations. Engineers view pilots as gung-ho, flashy show-boaters with little or no understanding of the mechanical and technical elements that enable them to fly. On the other side of the fence, pilots view engineers as anti-social beings who just want something to fix. That is not me propagating these stereotypes, just what I have experienced! Humorous typecasting aside, there is a huge amount of respect between these two parties. Having met with engineers in my recreational flying, and also through my work, I have a lot of time and respect for their knowledge and insight. They are highly educated and qualified professionals who are just as passionate about aviation and aircraft as the pilots who operate them are. If you are able to organise a visit and this point is all that you are able to take away from it, then you have not wasted your time. Knowing that the engineers are so heavily invested in aviation too inspires a great deal of confidence as a pilot. Furthermore, showing an interest in their work will help to develop that ever-important relationship.

In Chapter 11, I mentioned the use of carburettor heat and how it is an item we are prompted to check but we may not necessarily understand what it is we are checking. Your knowledge of what you are achieving when applying carburettor heat will develop over time through your application of it in flight and observing its subsequent effect, and from what you read of it in your manual. But to have the opportunity to view the part and its mechanics will serve to consolidate that knowledge. The manuals are written to provide an overview of its function and how it operates. To have an experienced and qualified engineer explain its operation can only lead to a better understanding.

Learning to fly is a real privilege, as you will have come to appreciate, and in the early stages of training your focus Is likely to be largely honed in on physically flying the aircraft. After all, this is where the majority of your satisfaction and early success will come from. However, there will come a time when you will need to also balance your 'hands-on' flying with preparation for your theoretical examinations.

Unlike being at school or college where exam dates ware set months in advance, when learning to fly the time scale in which to complete the nine theoretical exams is purely down to you as the student to set and manage. You are able to study and prepare as much, or as little, as you want and need, in your own time. The only 'gotcha' is that your progress through the flying syllabus is likely to stall if you delay completing your exams. I highlighted earlier my delay in completing the technical examinations; the Aircraft General Knowledge and the Principles of Flight exams. Fortunately, these topics did not hinder my flying progress, but there are some key topics that will bring your training to a halt, or potentially cost you further flying hours. By this, I mean you will be unable to continue with the syllabus but will instead have to spend money on a 'revision' flight just to maintain a level of proficiency – money better spent on progressing through the syllabus! One may argue that hours are hours and will contribute to your PPL; however, if you are looking to complete your training on a budget, or in the minimum time of 45 hours, then it would be worth completing the exams in good time ahead of key milestones in your training.

Relating this scenario to my training period – as I was approaching my navigation phase there was another student who was slightly younger than me but a lot further through the syllabus. He was due to complete his solo cross-country qualifying flight – an important milestone. The day before he was due to depart, the club called him and asked that he complete at least a couple of examinations before they authorised him to fly solo (as he had only completed two up to this stage). He had not been studying or revising and did not want to sit the exams because of this, so he was not authorised to complete his cross-country qualifying flight. He returned to university the following week and did not fly again until several months later. This pause in his flying meant that once he had passed his examinations he had to have a general handling revision lesson and had to fly the cross-country qualifying route, again, dual with an instructor, before being authorised to fly solo. This added a further three and a half hours to his training record and would have added around an extra £600 (660 €*) to his training costs. Again, it depends what your view point is on accumulating hours.

---

*   Exchange rate £1 = 1.10 € (Winter 2018)

With this in mind, I think it is important to set out a plan of how to complete your examinations and what level of priority you should assign them. The list I have produced below is not an authoritative order list – complete them in whatever order you deem fit. Your club may already have mapped out a route and revision schedule for you, perhaps. However, through experience, and through other pilots I have met, when you ask which exams to prioritise your club are likely to say, 'all of them.'

1 – Air Law.
2 – Human Performances.

Your club are likely to require you to pass these two examinations ahead of your solo flight. Study for these while training in the circuit.

3 – Meteorology.
4 – Aircraft General Knowledge.
5 – Aeroplane Technical.
6 – Operational Procedures.

You should aim to complete these four in one sitting (if you are able) while you are learning mixed circuits, practice forced landings and steep turns – this will be soon after your first solo and before your navigation exercises. Completing these subjects is not essential at this stage, but this period before your navigation training is an ideal time to complete them. It will also help to remove pressure towards the end of the syllabus when you are focusing on refining your flying skills.

7 – Air Navigation.

8 – Flight Planning and Performance.

Before you begin your dual navigation exercises your club/instructor will give you a navigation brief that will provide you with the fundamentals of the navigation and flight planning elements. Performance is likely to be a subject you will need to self-brief on but the content to consult can be found in *The Air Pilot's Manual 4: The Aeroplane – Technical.* You should aim to have the above complete by the time of your solo qualifying cross-country flight. It was the Air Navigation exam and the examinations number four to six on the list that brought my fellow student's training to a halt.

9 – VFR Communications (and the Radiotelephony Oral Test, soon after).

The radio communication exams are best kept until last. This will allow you greater exposure to the use of the radio before you undertake the assessment. The VFR Communications multi-choice exam has to be completed before your oral test. I would advise consulting the *Radiotelephony Manual –CAP 413* if you are a UK-based student or one of the similar publications mentioned in chapter 15 to allow you to be fully briefed ahead of the oral test. This topic will be addressed in a later chapter.

To conclude this chapter, I would like to bring to your attention and develop your thoughts on a relatively new initiative that is becoming increasingly popular in the EASA system. Many schools now offer a ground school tuition service, usually around £20-£30 (22-33 €) per session. These are likely to be led by the chief flying instructor or, perhaps, the instructor you fly with. I have found in my discussions with various pilots and students throughout their journey that this topic is rather divisive and controversial. In the USA, ground school is a required element of the Part 141 and Part 61 syllabuses. However, under the EASA syllabus ground school is not a required component for the issue of the licence – only the successful completion of the theoretical examinations.

Some flying schools may try to encourage you to join a study session and are likely to push the social reward of doing so. After all, it is a good way to meet other students and likeminded individuals. However, if you are aiming to complete your PPL on a budget, this additional expenditure can be avoided. Ultimately, it is up to you to decide and assess what kind of learner you are. If you are an independent learner who can learn from books and their own resources then I would say politely decline. However, if, on the other hand, you are a student who may need some additional support, and who may not have sound background knowledge in aviation, then maybe the ground school tuition is the perfect solution to your ground exam woes. Your flying school will likely assume you have conducted some independent study and will look to clarify topics you have struggled with – that is to say your tutor will not re-dictate the content of the flying manuals but will rather address subject matter that is not 'sticking'.

Similar to ground school tuition sessions, some flying schools offer a one-week *ab-initio* crash course that includes the delivery of the ground theory content and the completion of the examinations. I would advise against this method if you are part of the majority of learners who take around a year to work through the flying syllabus and gain the licence. I expect the crash courses market is for those who are looking to complete their PPL in a short period; however, with that said, it is still manageable to learn the content for the ground theory exams in the period that it takes to gain the minimum 45 hours required for the skills test. These five-day courses tend to market for around £800-£1,000 (880-1100 €). This price can double if you seek out a one-on-one learning experience. I have read reviews from both sides of the fence on these crash courses. These have varied from students exclaiming they would not have been able to complete the examinations without the course, to some customers implying the courses do not offer value for money and that they include no original material. I have offered my thoughts and those of other pilots here, but it is seminal to your journey that you self-assess your ability and requirement for support, if needed.

A s discussed, your first lessons will be a phased introduction to new skills, with the instructor delegating more responsibility to you with each successive lesson. By around your tenth flying hour, and at the very least before your first solo flight, you will have been introduced to all the fundamental flying skills such as take-off, landing, climbing turns, cruise, descending turns etc, all of which are elementary components in the circuit. However, being proficient with these skills is not sufficient criteria for your club and instructor to authorise you to fly solo.

In the previous chapter, the importance of the ground examination and the required dedication you must show was highlighted. To authorise your first solo flight, your club is likely to require you to complete a ground examination. This is not exclusively the case, but by this stage your training school will likely begin to apply pressure regarding your exams. My training school insisted I complete Air Law and Human Performances first (as per the previous chapter) before being set free into the circuit. I understood the need for the Air Law exam to be completed – having a pass in Air Law would indicate my proficiency in handling the aircraft within the legal parameters of the airspace I was operating in. On the other hand, I thought Human Performances was just another exam I could complete any time, but important nonetheless. I realise now, in hindsight, sitting these two exams at about a quarter of the way through my training, also played a second role as a pacemaker, set by the club, with the purpose of encouraging me to push forward with the theory to allow me to fly solo. This insistence on completing these first two exams prior to going solo also set the time frames and periods in which I should expect to sit the next batch of examinations, should my training continue to move at the pace it was moving at.

The Air Law subject matter can appear quite heavy going and by reading the pertinent section in *The Air Pilot's Manual 2: Air Law & Meteorology* you will come to realise there are many wide-spanning areas that the content covers, from airspace, aerodromes, licencing and rules of the air, to ICAO terminology, to name but a few. With this highlighted, I would advise learning and revising this subject first. By comparison, Human Performances is less dense and relate more to common sense.

A good student will begin studying the theory weeks in advance – though some schools suggest in advance of even starting your flight training! I feel this measure is unwarranted, as if you do start reading a content-heavy subject such as Air Law before any flying instruction, much of the content will be out of context and be wasted on you at such an early stage. Alluding earlier to a good student starting their learning weeks in advance...a time-pressured or disorganised student could learn the entirety of the subject comfortably in a week or, under cramming conditions, in a weekend if they are undisturbed. In reality, you are likely to see the same 100 or so questions come up out of the potentially endless span of information compressed into the Air Law chapters. Having access to a question bank or past papers will assist in guiding you towards the relevant content matter. WARNING – this is not to say that you do not need to read the entire Air Law manual. I would strongly advise any student to read it through in its entirety and give it the time and understanding it deserves.

However, it is possible to pass the real exam without reading the books and by sitting mock exams from question banks. But here are some good reasons why you should not:

1. You may be blindsided by a question you have not learned the answer to.
2. The real examination is likely to be in a different format with pencil and paper; this can influence performance.
3. There will be gaps in your knowledge that will catch you out, eventually.
4. You will feel less confident in your ability and knowledge as a pilot knowing you bypassed an important aspect of your training.
5. In rare circumstances, some question and answers lifted from question banks have been wrong.

The reasons stated above are examples that I, or fellow students, have fallen victim to. To elaborate on point 3 – I chose not to learn the marshalling signals as I knew they rarely appeared in the real examination and the airfield I flew from did not employ marshalling signals in their operation. From these two justifications, I thought I would not need that particular element of knowledge in my skill set. As expected, marshalling signals did not make an appearance in my examination. Fast forward six months, I was left rather red faced when I visited a new airfield on my qualifying cross-country qualification. With my instructor next to me, I did not know any of the marshalling signals. Rather than continue on the taxiway as their signal suggested, I instead interpreted their signal as 'direct to me' so I deviated from the taxiway. If that was not novice enough, once near the marshaller, for a second time I misinterpreted their signal by turning left when they were signalling right.

I dare not speculate what percentage of content matter actually appears in the Air Law examination question bank rotation. However, what I will highlight is that the content that is omitted from the rotation is not done so because it is any less important or pertinent to safety than the questions that do appear. You will feel a better student, and pilot, in the knowledge that you fulfilled not only an expectation, but a duty that comes with learning to fly an aircraft.

Human Performances is a great exam (and pass) to get early on in your training. It is a far more diluted subject in comparison to Air Law. This is a subject that can be overcome with little stress – many of the questions are common sense and you will find yourself laughing at some of the seemingly ridiculous options for answers. Though, I would advise you to learn the content attentively. By this I mean understand the difference between hypothermia and hyperthermia as the prefix-based questions are likely to catch you out. Another area to focus on is pilot condition-based questions; put yourself in the scenario and relate to your previous experiences. For example, in the dark, did the bright object appear closer or further away? These are the kind of questions that are likely to appear. Whereas Air Law can be quite dull and, metaphorically speaking, deep, Human Performances is a lighter subject, and one which you should be able to relate to. I think it is because of their vast differences that they are quite complimentary examinations to sit together.

f gaining a Private Pilot's Licence has been a long-held objective of yours then you may have considered the use of a flight simulator to gently nurture your interests. In this chapter, I want to discuss the use of a flight simulator as a training tool and what advantages and drawbacks these kinds of software can offer.

Personally, I used flight simulation software in my earlier days when real flight was not as accessible. During the period I used a flight simulator, and main products on the market were Microsoft Flight Simulator X (FSX) and XPlane. Those familiar with flight simulation will be aware of these products. More recent versions of XPlane have seen the development of the flight and performance modelling. Whilst, on the other hand, FSX has seen a more recent incarnation as Prepar3d, or P3D; a development from its predecessor spearheaded by Lockheed Martin after their acquisition of Microsoft's intellectual property. There are discussions to be had about the bad habits that using a flight simulator can instil in a student. Being someone who frequently used this means of emulating flying and then went on to gain a PPL, I feel as though I can comfortably assess this tool. Being the optimist that I am, I will begin first with assessing the positives of flight simulation software.

The first main advantage to using a flight simulator is the exposure it gives you to a standard cockpit configuration. Even the most basic aircraft on a simulator will include the primary flight instruments that you will be familiar with seeing in the cockpit of your basic trainer aircraft. From the safety of your computer, you can practice manoeuvres and see their effect on the instrumentation. Pulling excessive-force manoeuvres that you would otherwise not attempt in a real aircraft would be a pointless exercise. However, the use of a simulator can help you become more proficient in interpreting your instruments. There are some accurate representations of real aircraft that can be purchased as additional content to better improve your simulator experience. A software developer by the name of Carenado has produced some highly accurate, light aircraft add-ons to largely include most of the basic trainer aircraft that a student would train on. These add-ons are compatible with the FSX, P3D and XPlane platforms.

Besides a familiarisation of aircraft interiors, a flight simulator also helps as a training tool with regards to airspace and airfield geography, which are both accurately represented. Periodic updates address any real world augmentation to the airfields and airspace. A flight simulator is a great way to learn about further airfields besides the ones you have visited during your flight training. In a simulation environment, you can fly to and from any airport in the world. Keeping it local, relatively speaking, the use of a simulator can aid your situational awareness i.e. knowing what airfields are near to you. Subliminally, while simulating flight from different airfields, you will learn the runway alignments and dimensions which can help in assessing their suitability in the real world. Even with just the default settings in place, most flight simulators accurately plot towns and major landmarks and are able to replicate coastlines – at least, in enough detail to comfortably navigate with. After-market products can be purchased that can improve the scenery to better emulate the real world environment. Such add-ons can accurately map roads, railways and rivers as well, precisely representing the density of buildings and woodland areas.

Just through 'playing' you are likely to stumble across more procedural flying. Though this is above and beyond the level of PPL flying, there is no harm in developing an appreciation for more advanced flying. While flying as a PPL pilot, it will greatly enhance your situational awareness and context, if you were to overhear and understand two-way conversation between an advanced pilot and an air traffic controller when discussing an instrument arrival, for example. While on the topic of advanced flying, later in your training you will be introduced to VHF Omnidirectional Range (VOR) tracking and dead-reckoning. A flight simulator is able to accurately represent this level of flying. It is likely you will be able to practice your VOR work on the same VOR you will use in your flight training.

Whenever there are positives, there will always be drawbacks to discuss – and the same applies with flight simulators.

Initially, I think it is important to note that whilst flight simulators have advanced considerably over the past decade, they cannot entirely replicate the real flight experience. Currently, P3D and XPlane vie for the accolade of best flight simulation experience. Compared to earlier flight simulators, their flight performance models are far more advanced. By flight performance model, I mean the ability for the simulator to replicate an aircraft's performance and behaviour in different environments and conditions. In your training, when approaching the runway, you will be introduced to setting your power to a reduced RPM, gently pulling on the yoke to hold the nose up in order to maintain altitude, deploy flaps if necessary, and then once approach speed is captured you would trim for that speed and begin the descent. However, I have found flight simulators find it difficult to replicate this kind of behaviour. I have tried the same procedure, as above, but instead of gently sinking and trying to maintain the same altitude by pulling the nose up slowly, in a flight simulator the aircraft instead climbs away. This power-attitude modelling, I find, is not accurately emulated. A further example would be when in straight and level flight – in a real aircraft if you were to adjust the power the aircraft would want to either climb or descend, based off your input. In a real-world environment, you would need to recapture your attitude and re-trim. However, in some simulators, if you increase the power, the speed simply increases and your altitude remains unchanged. Computer models, whilst advanced, are limited by binary restrictions (0101 computer coding for us lay people). To that end, computer modelling will always struggle to replicate the seemingly fluid nature of our environment.

The familiarisation of aircraft instruments was discussed earlier; however, there is also a drawback to this exposure. For the purpose of the PPL, student pilots are taught to be VFR pilots and fly the aircraft by looking out. A PPL pilot should only need to reference their instruments for speed and altitude periodically. The excessive use of a flight simulator can get you into the bad habit of continuously looking at your instruments rather than looking outside the aircraft and maintaining a good look out. Whilst using a flight simulator, the grave risk of an aircraft collision is not a concern. Furthermore, the external environment of a flight simulator is less stimulating than real flying, so you could find yourself constantly monitoring and assessing your simulated instruments. These behaviours then make it to the cockpit. I remember during one of my first lessons, my instructor guessed correctly that I had been using a flight simulator by my constant fixation on the aircraft instruments. Their solution was to conceal the instruments with a high visibility jacket in order to focus my attention outside of the aircraft. It seemed drastic at first, as I felt as though I needed to reference the instruments constantly. However, sure enough, this habit subsided and soon I became comfortable knowing I was flying straight and level by looking at the horizon.

Besides bad habits and slightly inaccurate flight modelling, flight simulation can be an expensive hobby. The basic product can cost around £50 (55 €*); however, to really improve the flight-simulation experience, you may need to purchase one of the many after-market products such as scenery upgrades, better represented

---

* Exchange rate £1 = 1.10 € (Winter 2018)

aircraft and, perhaps, computer hardware upgrades. I spoke to a flight simulator YouTuber who advised that to achieve a flight simulation experience that was as smooth running and looked as realistic as could be tangibly possible, an enthusiast would need to spend upwards of £2,000 (2,200 €*) on computer hardware and flight simulation software. During your training, this kind of money is best spent on your actual flight training, I feel!

I n a hypothetical world, you have been handed an object that you have no knowledge of. All the resources you need to assist your learning have been made available to you. You have been tasked with grasping the fundamental skills and techniques of it. You have three months. Three months, you would argue, is plenty of time to overcome the early stumbling points and minor hurdles to grasp a basic command of a skill. I have met people who have been able to learn French to a basic conversational standard within that time period. Many aspiring guitarists can pick up a guitar for the first time on a Monday and be able to strum along to their favourite song by the end of the week. The difference between, say, learning a language or to play guitar and learning to fly an aircraft is a matter of availability and access.

I used three months as this is roughly the time frame it would take a student to reach solo standard, at around 10-15 hours, assuming that the student is flying 3-4 times a month. Continuing on with the guitar example, accumulating 10-15 hours of experience can be achieved easily over the course of a week, and quite possibly over the course of a weekend (much like your Air Law!). Admittedly, the guitarist should not expect to be highly skilled after 15 hours of playing, but they should, however, expect a noted increase in skill and execution. The same applies to flying; however, the differences lies in the currency of proficiency. As a student pilot you may gain three to four hours 'hands-on' experience a month, perhaps. A student guitarist could achieve the same amount of learning in a morning before lunch. The noted pauses between your flights will be evident in your flying. You will notice the impact on your proficiency less if you are able to fly at regular intervals. Flying once a week, you will maintain a good level of hands-on skill and capability. If you then pause for three weeks, I am confident you will notice a decline in your ability to jump straight back into the aircraft and operate it to the standard you were flying three weeks previously. Albeit, at least for the first few minutes.

Around the time of your solo flight you want to have the best level of proficiency available to you before being released. As it is not possible to simply jump in an aircraft and hone the skill of flying the circuit whenever you have a spare half hour on a Tuesday evening, try 'armchair flying'. This is likely to be a phrase you would have heard, if not from your instructor, at least from other students around your flying club. The idea, essentially, is to sit in a chair and simulate flying the circuit. Not necessarily in real time if you are time restricted, but at a pace whereby you can simulate running through the various stages of flight. You may argue that in your armchair you are unable to simulate the effects of weather phenomena such as wind and visibility. Whilst this is true, this is not the point of armchair flying. Only 'on the day' are you able to assess and interact with the given weather phenomena. After all, twisting your imaginary yoke in and out of wind and planting your left foot to the carpet will only serve to make you feel silly and will not serve your judgement and assessment of the conditions when you do eventually fly. That will come down to experience through exposure.

Find yourself somewhere quiet to sit and have your checklist to hand, as, in part, the purpose of armchair flying is to master your fluidity and timings of your checklist. Besides becoming smooth with your checklist procedure, it will assist you in becoming familiar with the quick reconfigurations of the aircraft that take place. In the space of roughly five minutes or so, you will reconfigure the aircraft from take-off to climb, climb to cruise, cruise to approach and approach to land, before streamlining the aircraft back to take-off capability and naturally repeating the process. By being able to run through your checklists accurately and quickly, it allows more time to focus on the handling, reconfiguring and manoeuvring of the aircraft. While in your armchair, run through the steps that do not appear in your checklist, such as your attitude–power–trim checks and knowing your critical speeds.

Your improving situational awareness will help you in your checklist procedure. If, when entering into the circuit, you can hear over the radio multiple aircraft in communication with the controller, and traffic information being called out, you can lessen your workload later on by completing your downwind checks slightly earlier than you would otherwise do. This will not impact on the safety of your flight, nor should it bring criticisms from your instructor as it displays good airmanship. You do not want to find yourself on your downwind leg attempting to keep visual separation from an aircraft ahead of you, trying to get your 'downwind' call in, then realising when turning to your base leg you have not completed your downwind checks. The key in a busy circuit pattern is to keep ahead of the aircraft and the situation by managing your workload.

A very useful bit of advice given to me after I completed my training was the use of YouTube videos in practising the circuit. In its simplest terms, you load a video of somebody flying a circuit, disregard their handling and radio communication, and instead in real-time work through your checklist and circuit procedure. If you are fortunate enough, you may be able to find a video of a pilot flying the circuit at the airfield you learn at. You will be able to find videos of aircraft entering busy circuit patterns and, true to the self-developing and improving nature of pilots, many of the content creators will provide a self-critique of their performance before inviting viewers to provide their feedback – positive and negative, but in terms that are constructive.

Enroute on a beautiful VFR day.

The world below looks at its best from 2,000 feet.

The colour of the land and sea can change vastly from season to season. It is certainly more noticeable from the air.

Taking a look under the engine cowling will
help your technical understanding.

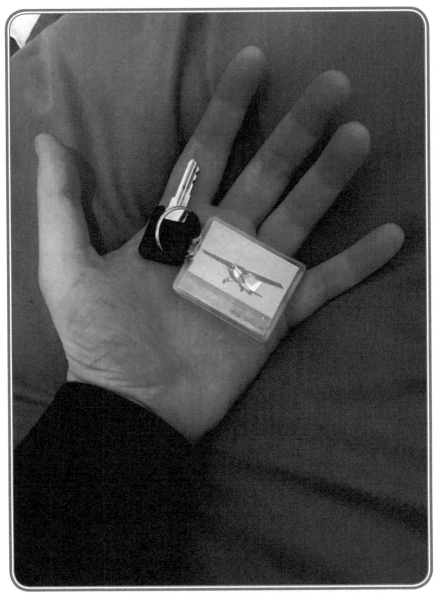

Top tip: do not take the aircraft keys home with you!

The flight computer may appear intimidating at first, but
with practice using it will become second nature.

A model aircraft used in flight schools to explain and
demonstrate aircraft flight surface systems.

The day all pilots look forward to:
the day their licence arrives in the mail.

S ome instructors may give you a heads up before your first solo, whilst others may keep it quiet and spring it upon you while you are flying in the circuit and then simply hop out on the taxiway. To best prepare yourself for going solo you must pick up on a few key giveaways. Being sent solo is something you should be anticipating and planning for. As such, if your instructor feels comfortable signing you off for a solo flight then you would have been clearly demonstrating a level of proficiency that inspires confidence from your instructor. This is important because, ultimately, your instructor is responsible at this stage whilst you are under training.

Firstly, if your instructor is continuing to provide positive feedback while flying in the circuit you can take that as a strong indicator of your upcoming solo flight. Whilst being told your overall flying and landings are good is a warm pleasantry, after a while your instructor may stay quiet. After all, there are only so many times you can expect to be complimented. If your instructor decides to hold an episode of silence while you are flying in the circuit, it usually suggests they are happy with your flying and are looking to adopt the 'hands-off' approach and leave you to fly the aircraft without direction. It took me a while to appreciate the silent treatment, but I now respect its importance in building independence and confidence in flying. In this instance, expect the only time an instructor would get involved is if the scenario you find yourself in exceeds your experience level or if the environment becomes unsuitable to comfortably instruct in.

On the ground and in advance of any flying, there may be some suggestion of your solo flight by means of commenting on the weather conditions. A talking point in most club environments is the weather, so if there are quite reassuring comments with regards to light wind and good visibility, especially from your instructor, then this could be a positive sign. Ideally, your club would look to send you solo for the first time when winds are calm or directly down the runway. Tackling a crosswind whilst also dealing with the adrenaline and anxiety of your first solo circuit is a lot to contend with; with that in mind, expect only to fly solo on a clear and calm day.

Nearer the time or even on the day of your prospective solo flight, you may find your club checking over your records to make sure all required exercises are complete. They may even ask to see your log book to check your completed exercises as per *The Air Pilot's Manual 1: Flying Training* against their records and the syllabus. To fly solo, you also need to hold of a current Class 2 Medical as covered in chapter nine, so you may be asked questions regarding this. Your club should have a copy of your medical certificate on file, but your instructor might ask just to check – this was a big hint for me.

In advance of the day, your instructor or club may advise booking in for a double slot – one in the morning, one in the afternoon. If you are a student who is only looking to fly once or twice a fortnight then this advice is again an indicator of a solo flight. With the two slots, your instructor is likely to spend time observing your standard landings; potentially showing you an orbit hold in the circuit; and teaching you emergency procedures such as rejected take-off or engine failure after take-off, allowing you time to develop an overall proficiency. Having two one-hour slots is plenty of time to achieve all of the above. The last 15 minutes of your second slot is likely when you will be sent solo. Variables outside of your control that may stop your solo flight being authorised are the deterioration of the weather conditions; a very busy traffic pattern; and technical/operational restrictions – i.e. an aircraft defect or airport closure.

The most important thing for your solo flight is to be mentally prepared. If you are the sort of person who does not give yourself credit for your achievements then you may think you are not ready – this is something I will discuss in a later chapter. It is a very surreal notion to compute – flying a plane by yourself – but remember your training will be managed in the hands of very experienced training professionals. What I found to be the most bizarre concept was how inexperienced and novice I felt, including the thought process of 'am I ready and am I really going to be trusted to do this?' I suppose having feelings of self-doubt proves that not only are you human but you also have the capacity to assess and analyse – very important skills for a pilot. By this, I mean to assess yourself, your ability, give credit where it is due and, of course, to highlight where you are not so strong. You will need to pause and reflect over the things you can do and that you have proven dozens of times already to your instructor. It is not as though you are being asked to demonstrate a task that you have not already completed many times before.

As mentioned at the beginning of this chapter, it is very much down to your club and instructor how they release you for a solo flight. You may be told outright at the beginning of the day that 'today will be the day', subject to weather and how busy the circuit is. On the other hand, they may not do this as to so as not to build up hope or anxiety – whatever of each is the most overriding emotion of the day. I suppose it is very much dependent on the student and how the club feels is the best way to manage their transition.

Another way for your solo to be offered to you is while you are in flight and introduced unexpectedly, perhaps as a test to see how you perform under pressure and a quick change of circumstance. This is how my solo flight was offered to me, as well as my good friend who was training at the same time.

The instructor will show you a number of emergency procedures, such as an engine failure after take-off and a rejected take-off. If the airfield at which you train is co-ordinated by air traffic control then, of course, this can only be demonstrated if it has capacity to do so and only once they authorise it. Usually after the simulated engine failure, and once on your downwind leg, the instructor will make a call for a full-stop landing and for a rejected take-off (you may have to vacate and re-enter if the runway is short). Once you land and then demonstrate a rejected take-off, the instructor will then ask you to vacate the runway and will make a call to air traffic control (or a blind call if non-controlled) to state their intention to send you solo. They will give a quick brief and ask if you are ready, then that is it.

You will be sitting there on the taxiway, no instructor, tasked with executing one circuit without in-flight supervision. There are two things usually that catch out freshly released solo students. The first thing is the call sign. Your instructor will inform you of your new prefix. Say, for example, your call sign with your instructor was 'G-ABCD', shortened to 'G-CD' – once sent solo you will have to report your status as a solo student by using the prefix 'Student'. So, in the example above, you will become 'Student G-ABCD', shortened to 'Student CD'. Do note, however, you may only use a shortened call sign after it has been shortened by the air traffic service you are interacting with. The second thing that catches out newly sent solo students is the change in aircraft performance. If you are training on a Cessna 152, your max take-off weight is circa 750kg, and after two hours of flying your fuel burnt brings your weight down to 690kg. Then your 80kg instructor leaves the aircraft. Your aircraft is now 20 per cent lighter than it was when you first departed. The aircraft becomes immediately 12 per cent lighter when your instructor exits the aircraft. This change in mass is evident when you lift-off on your solo flight. As soon as you rotate, the aircraft's climb performance is improved and it is very noticeable – the aircraft leaps for the sky. Once at the top of climb, you may notice less RPM is needed to maintain the cruise speed. Overall, the aircraft feels more sporting, agile and responsive with less mass on-board.

With any luck, you will make a great job of the landing. Your instructor will be watching from a viewing area or the tower, but try not to let that affect your performance. Once parked, you will no doubt be feeling ecstatic and your instructor will meet and congratulate you. If you have brought friends and family I am sure this will be the time when photos can be taken. Most flying schools now take photos of their students after their first solo flight and share them on social media. In some flying circles, largely in the United States of America, it is tradition to cut off the tail or lower back of the shirt being worn. This tradition derives from the era when training was conducted in open cockpit tandem trainers, with the student sat ahead of the instructor. Before radios, the instructor would tug on the tail of the student's shirt to gain their attention. Therefore, the cutting of the shirt indicates the student can fly without an instructor, though this tradition is less observed in Europe. Of course, there is a lot of instruction still to follow, as you, as a student, move from the basic handling qualities and towards the more refined airmanship skills and techniques required to be a well-rounded pilot.

Having gone solo, you have become a pilot in some definition, albeit not a qualified pilot yet. It does mean, however, you are able to write your name in your log book under Commander for the first time and that is, indeed, a very special occasion.

26

A t stages throughout flight training there are often natural breaks where you may take pauses in your training. Post-solo is one of those times where you may want to pause. In the not-so-distant future, after your first solo, you will move onto the navigation element of the syllabus; this period of training can be more costly as it involves longer flying periods as your one-hour local flight becomes one-and-a-half to two-hour cross-country flights. Having just gone solo you may ask why would I want to take a break from flying now? Well, if you have the money set aside you may not need to. However, if you are paying lesson by lesson, at this stage it might be a good time to take a short break in training and save some money so as to not cause later disruptions.

If you were to take a pause and not fly solo for a month or two, your levels of proficiency will naturally drop somewhat, but an hour or two with an instructor will remedy that. Also, having gone solo, it does not now mean that all future flights will be solo. You will still need your 25 hours of dual instruction. After going solo, do not expect your subsequent flights to be more of the same.

Quite possibly your next two bookings will be 'mixed' circuits or a local flight tackling steep turns and stalling. You will still have the opportunity to land the aircraft in your dual instruction lessons. Most of your solo hours will come from navigation work later in the syllabus. Also, if you are focussed on gaining your PPL within 45 hours, it is still possible with pauses. I gained my licence in 45 hours with two pauses – factored within the 45-hour syllabus are revision flights that can be used for that purpose. One of those said pauses was after my cross-country qualifier, which brought me up to the 10 solo hours. I did not fly solo again for the rest of my training, which took a further eight months to complete.

Having moved on from your first solo, your time spent in the circuit will continue but this time looking at mixed circuits, as mentioned earlier. Mixed circuits include looking at power-off glide approaches, flapless landings and short-field full flap landings (if you do not do these already). After a couple of sessions looking at these techniques, you will be released to practice these solo in the circuit. This is likely to be your second solo hour in your log book. In my experience I flew two glide, two flapless and two short-field landings in this hour. The difference between short-field and standard in my experience was a third and final stage of flap. The reason for these mixed (or varied) circuits as it provides you with experience and exposure to non-standard approaches that simulate engine failure as demonstrated in the glide and electronic failure as demonstrated in the flapless approach. If training at an airfield with a sizeable runway, the short-field landing technique is taught for future flying – in and out of smaller aerodromes – as well as for practice forced landings in the event of an engine failure in flight, where you may be left with no option but to land in a small field.

Now, much later in this chapter than originally planned, I want to revisit landings. You may wonder why, at this stage, this far into this guide, would the author want to discuss landing technique? I would forgive you for asking that question, but quite surprisingly it is at this stage of training that some students, in some form, *forget* how to land the aircraft.

Most bizarre, right?

How, at this stage, when a student has demonstrated their proficiency by flying an aircraft unsupervised in the cockpit, could they forget how to land the plane, forgetting everything they have learned?

Again, it is that word – proficiency. This does not happen to everyone but it can creep up on students later on in their training and it happens for a very logical reason.

Follow me through this scenario. In your earlier training, pre-solo, you spent many hours in the circuit practising normal, standard approaches and landings. In a one-hour session, you may have flown eight circuits. The first two landings might have been a little rough around the edges, and the remaining ones were a mix of very good to average. You walked away having demonstrated at least four good landings out of eight and, of course, you will always remember the good ones…Fast forward a couple of months – you have gone solo, you have then practised varied circuits dual and solo for a couple of hours and now, you move onto steep-turns in the local area away from the aerodrome. You are then tasked to land the aircraft normally in standard conditions. What can, and may, happen is that that landing will be a bit sloppy, but you let that one slide… Two weeks later you fly again and the same thing happens for a second time. Suddenly, your confidence drops – a couple of months ago you were flying great in the circuit and then, subsequently, flew solo, and now you are struggling to pull off a standard approach into an airfield that you have landed at 30-40+ times. What has gone wrong?

Well, you can see clearly with hindsight, that in this scenario the student has not flown a normal approach since their solo flight; they have been introduced to three new landing techniques and practised those intensely. They have then produced two poor normal landings, back-to-back, two weeks apart – does that mean they have forgotten how to land the plane? Well, no, it is likely because of a lack of practice and proficiency. Remember back to when the student was in the circuit. It is likely they executed more landings in that one hour than they did in the following two months. That said, in the circuit, their first two circuit landings were poor but the rest were fine. They would not have had the time to dwell and mull over the poor landings as they were straight back into the circuit and had another attempt – subsequently producing a good landing. Time has a fascinating effect on the brain. Those two poor landings, two weeks apart, may impact the student's confidence.

I experienced this later in my training during my dual cross-country navigation routes – three landings over three flights were poor.

You never know what conditions you will experience on a day – both environmentally and personally. By my third flight, I felt as though I was owed a good landing. I ensured I was well rested, relaxed and prepared for flight and was elated to see the conditions were perfect – the landing was poor. It just was not my day. Just because I had two bad landings before did not mean the world owed me a perfect third landing. Ironically, it was during the following flight when visibility was poor and I had left my water bottle on the ground, both of which affected my concentration, that I produced a good landing.

I worked out that my proficiency was the issue when looking back at my log book after the event. I am sure if I had discussed my concern about landings with my instructor they would have identified the lack of standard approaches and proficiency levels associated with it. It is important to discuss your concerns with your instructor if this happens. They may even suggest returning to the airfield early while out flying to practice a few landings. In a way, it is much like golf. You can purchase 100 balls for the driving range and end up miscuing them left and right. But when you connect sweetly with that *one* ball, you forget the other 99.

I f your training were to be scripted as a play or film then the weather would likely land the role of the antagonist. Whilst meteorologists are able to forecast 48 hours of weather with improved reliability through mesoscale modelling and numerical weather predictions, weather is still very much a law unto itself and can rapidly change or deteriorate without it being expected to.

As a soon-to-be qualified pilot, the decision to launch is down to you as commander; if you are renting a club aircraft, the club are likely to also have an input on this judgement. To be able to quantify and sensibly picture what the weather is doing from the current observation and future forecasts is a seminal skill that a pilot needs to be able to minimise risk. I mention both the current observation and future forecast as there is little sense in setting off now in good conditions if you know that the weather is going to deteriorate considerably around the time of your arrival, either back to your home base or to an onward destination. Within the vicinity of the airfields, these observations and forecasts are known as METAR and TAF, respectively. METAR is an acronym for

Meteorological **A**erodrome **R**eport and TAF represents **T**erminal **A**erodrome **F**orecast. These reports largely follow the same format and use the same codes to detail and denote the weather.

So, as a student, how do you go about painting this image of the weather? I will explain the steps I was shown as a student. These steps were so logical and applicable that I still use them now as part of my self-brief when flying:

1 – In the days leading up to a lesson, keep your eye on the weather via the news. These visuals and explanations are more interactive than what you will find in written format on the internet or in the newspapers. They will show you the moving pressure systems and air masses and should give a forecast as to how they are expected to behave in the coming days. We usually associate cold and low air pressure masses with poor conditions, so they are important to monitor. The more generalised comments like 'it will be windy across most parts heading into the weekend' can also assist in laying the basic foundation to your 'image'.

2 – On the morning of your lesson, open the curtains and take a look outside or step outside your front door. Gauge what the weather is doing where you are, as it could be indicative of the wider weather patterns. Try to get a feel for the wind, clouds and visibility. Look and listen for the wind –are the trees rustling aggressively? Is there small debris blowing down the street? Can you hear the wind howling? Are the clouds, if there are

any, moving fast through the sky? And with regards to clouds, are they sitting low, roughly below 1,000 feet? Are they dark and look as if they are holding precipitation? Is there extended vertical development of cumulonimbus clouds indicative of a storm cell? Now, onto visibility – does the sky look clear? Can you gauge the visual range against the distance of objects you know?

On a good day, you would expect clear skies, calm winds and good visual range, naturally.

3 – Check general weather reports to see if there are any specific weather phenomena that may affect flight in the area you are looking to operate. Strong winds, storms etc.

4 – If the overall weather picture from non-specialised reports appear positive then begin consulting aviation specific weather reports. Begin with the departing aerodromes METAR/TAF. The METAR and TAF will produce a more detailed report of the aerodrome's weather observation and forecast tailored to its immediate and surrounding geographical position. For example, winds may be calm in the town nearby; however, if the airfield is situated on a peninsula close to the sea, the winds may be vastly different. If the weather appears good at the departure aerodrome then start looking at the arrival aerodrome, if applicable. Check it in this order as there is no point checking the arrival aerodrome

weather if it is highly unlikely you are going to be able to get out of the departing aerodrome in the first place!

I will refrain from going into the explanation of the METAR/TAF and the associated coding as that is specialised knowledge that will need to be taught by your instructor or learned through your training manuals. However, I will give an overview of a random METAR from Gatwick and the picture I would take away from it:

METAR: EGKK 111350Z 14004KT 110V180 9999 FEW016 09/05 Q1024

Initial thoughts are that winds are calm but variable in direction; visibility is good; clouds are at a sensible dispersion and height; temperature and dew point are adequately separated so there is little risk of fog; and pressure is moderate – this is a positive observation and would suit PPL flying.

TAF: EGKK 111057Z 1112/1118 10005KT 9999 FEW035 TEMPO 1202/1209 7000

The TAF reads that between 1200 and 1800 today winds will be a light breeze with good visibility and clouds interspersed at 3500 feet. It does advise, however, that from 0200-0900 the following day, visibility will reduce to 7,000m. For a private pilot, VFR visibility minimums in uncontrolled airspace is 5,000m. Personally, I choose not to fly in anything less than 7,000m, reported. Through experience, you will be able to quantify your own personal minimums. A way to do so is by remembering the value of a visual range that made you feel uncomfortable while learning to fly and had you thinking 'I would not want to fly through this without an instructor'.

5 – The last of the aviation specific weather reports I consult are the low-level weather and spot winds reports across a given region. The low-level weather chart is less detailed than the METAR and TAF but will give an overview on larger weather systems and their associated phenomena. Also included in this document will be information relating to icing and turbulence. The latter document is of particular use in relation to calculating your ground speed for cross-country flying.

Once I have consulted all five of these means of determining the weather, I deem myself fully briefed. It is designed to start with a basic forecast and progress through the layers of detail. As such, if by stage three I am adequately satisfied that flying will not go ahead – for example, because there is a three-day storm bringing winds of 60 knots – I do not move onto the following stages.

Having a good grip and understanding of the weather is testament to a good pilot and will earn you praise from your club and other pilots when making the right call. Safety is such a central theme in general aviation that you are likely to receive more praise and respect for making the decision not to launch in testing conditions than you would if you took the ill-decision and got airborne. Ironically, you will likely garner a reputation of being a gambler and risk taker rather than the intended romantic and idealised image of being thought of as an heroic, cream-of-the-crop pilot who took on the weather and won…this time.

A s a direct lead on from mastering the weather basics, it would be sensible to also spend a short period giving some thought to how the weather affects the aircraft's performance.

An aircraft flying through the sky is much akin to a ship sailing on water, albeit on an additional plane. You may have seen a ship sailing through the water appearing to be almost sailing sideways. A ship's course can be affected by a current, and this is not too dissimilar to the way an aircraft flies in a crosswind. There will be a time in your training when you will be asked to track an object, for example, a tower. But as you get closer it appears to keep moving off to the side, so you will continue turning towards it and the below demonstrates, pictorially, what will happen:

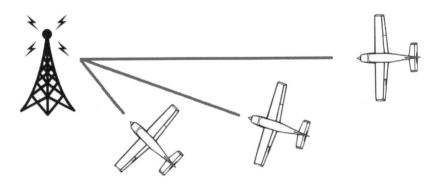

This will be the result of continually trying to track the object by placing it on the nose of your aircraft. On a day with calm skies and no wind, placing the object on the nose will achieve the goal of arriving overhead said object, but more often than not you will have some wind to contend with. This scenario is a good lesson in understanding the impact of wind and wind corrections in order to successfully track inbound to an object. See again the image but this time showing the wind vector.

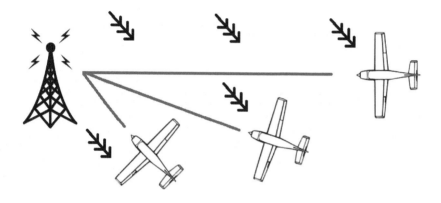

Note how the aircraft nearest the tower is travelling directly into wind. Only at this stage will the object remain fixed on the aircraft nose should no flight control alterations be made.

To be able to track inbound to an object, without constantly altering the heading, is an important skill to master and to also appreciate. For example, in the above scenario, if I were to draw the aircraft's track, you will see it has followed an elliptical flight path. This is undesired and should be avoided, especially in the case of controlled airspace and restricted/danger areas.

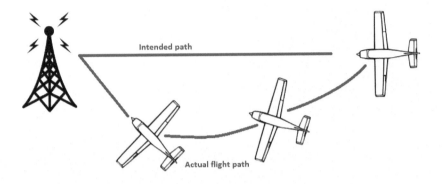

Whilst this kind of flying can be forgiven during your training period, being able to gauge and feel for the wind is an important airmanship skill to refine. With experience, you will get the feel for the wind and will be able to account for the drift. If the object keeps drifting to the right as you try to track it, as it has done in this example, aim past the object to its right, keeping the object to your left. You will see that you will be able to track the object more accurately with less correction.

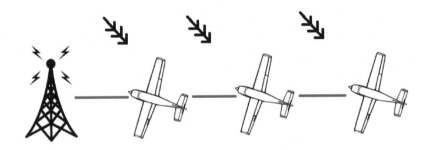

Of course, with the object now off to left, this phenomenon can lead you to think that you will pass by the object entirely. However, if gauged correctly you will arrive directly overhead your target.

See below an image you would expect to see from the cockpit with annotations.

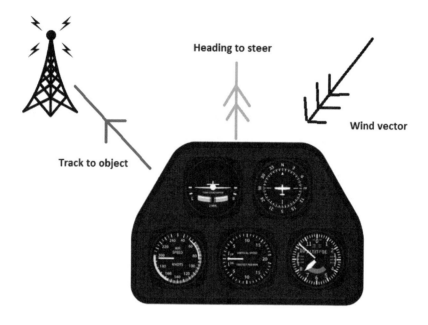

The difference between the track to the object and the heading to steer is known as the wind correction angle. To calculate your heading to steer you must have a wind vector to input, a true airspeed, and a track to follow. A simple representation of this is shown below using our aforementioned scenario.

The single arrow is the track we want to follow; the triple arrow is the wind vector affecting the aircraft's desired track; and the double arrow is the heading we must steer to achieve the track – you can see how in triangular form the heading to steer is a balance between the track and the wind vector. These calculations will be covered in your navigation brief as well as through tuition on your flight computer.

In flight, it is not easy to verify the wind. Yet, nature and the immediate environment can provide some rudimental clues. These can be observed by monitoring cloud movement, the directions of waves in the sea, smoke columns, visible flags etc.

n order for you to have gone solo you would have needed a current, and in-date, VFR chart for the region you fly in. The most common scale is the 1:500,000. So if you are flying solo from Dunkeswell in the United Kingdom, you would need the 1:500,000 Southern England and Wales. Similarly, if you were flying from Friedrichshafen in Germany, you would require the Stuttgart 1:500,000 scale chart.

With the navigation element of the syllabus fast approaching, it would be wise to become familiar with your local area, as depicted on your chart. If you are already geographically aware of your surroundings then great! You are likely then to already have a good idea of what towns surround your training airfield, where they are located and what distinguishing features they have to aid your navigation. If not, all the information you need to safely navigate will be expressed on your chart. The VFR charts can be quite congested, dotted with colour and can, quite ironically, be rather difficult to navigate! Included on the chart will be the names of towns and cities – the larger the settlements the larger the font. The settlement's outline is drawn to give an indication of its shape and where the concentrations of buildings give way to the countryside. Motorways and arterial roads are mapped out much like a road atlas; these are very useful navigation aids and many pilots will navigate between destinations by following the existing road networks, or at least by referencing them.

The first thing that struck me with this scale of chart is how close towns and visual reference points appear to one another. It gave the illusion that these points were very close to one another, they would be hard to tell apart and I would travel between them at great speed which would lead to identification problems...What appears close on the paper chart will, in fact, be a considerable distance in reality when looking out of the cockpit. After all, on this scale chart one centimetre represent five kilometres. So, what would appear as 1.5 centimetres on a chart will equate to 7.5 kilometres, which, in turn, might take three minutes or so to travel. In light of this, towns and visual points will not be approaching you so speedily that you will not have time to manage your navigation, fly the plane and communicate with air traffic control. Also, a quick rule of thumb with these charts is exactly that: a rule for the thumb. If a navigation ruler ever evades you in the cockpit, know that the distance between the end of the thumb and its joint (around 2.5cm) roughly equates to 10 nautical miles.

While becoming familiar with your local area on your VFR chart, spend some time looking further afield from your base as you may come across features that may not be prevalent in your area of operation. I was discouraged from looking further than my area as my chart was folded in such a particular way I dared not unravel it! In hindsight, that would have been a small price to pay. There were many navigational features I had not seen, including military zones and areas of intense aerial activity (AIAA), the latter of which caused much confusion when flying with a friend for the first time. We were flying through uncontrolled airspace so were under no obligation to talk to a controller. We were near a military zone that could offer a basic service using their radar, but we elected not to use it. Soon after, a message appeared on my friend's GPS to say we had entered the military installation's radar zone. Needless to say, we made an abrupt U-turn and began consulting our chart. It turned out that we had not actually entered a controlled zone but we had crossed a boundary denoted by a diamond line. When we checked the key, we learned that the diamond line represented an AIAA, and whilst there was not anything stopping us crossing that line, the key also read that 'pilots are strongly advised to make contact with the radar service provider'. I had not seen a feature like this in the area of the chart I was more familiar with, largely owing to a lack of military zones in the part of the country I learned to fly in.

In conclusion, demonstrating a good level of competency with your chart will go a long way in keeping you safe. Especially so now that many pilots have transitioned from their paper charts to relying on GPS to tell them they are on track and that airspace is approaching. Whilst they are still legally obligated to carry their VFR chart with them, many only do so to fulfil that obligation and do not reference it at all, instead putting their safe navigation in to the precarious hands of technology. If/when the technology fails you, knowing how to interpret your chart will put you in good stead for a safe return.

n relation to the VFR chart and controlled airspace, it is important to be able to visualise the airspace in a three-dimensional plane to avoid infringing on an aerodrome's control zone. Included on the VFR charts will be the altitudes in which the controlled airspace is in operation. So long as your altitude remains outside of these parameters you are able to pass freely under or over a block of controlled airspace. See the below visual for a representation of an aerodrome's control zone:

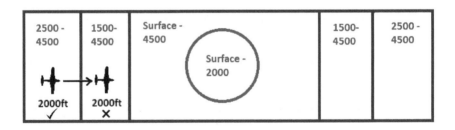

In this diagram, which is similar to what would appear on a VFR chart, the aircraft is flying at 2,000 feet. On first inspection, it looks as though the aircraft is flying in controlled airspace. However, as the aircraft is operating at an altitude that is outside of the 2500-4500 feet parameter, the aircraft is free to operate and remains outside of controlled airspace. However, if the aircraft then continues on its path, it will proceed to encroach on the block of controlled airspace between 1500-4500 feet.

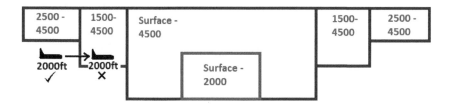

This is, perhaps, easier to view if we were to observe the same in-flight scenario from a cross sectional, side-on perspective.

Albeit the aircraft in the first position is outside of the controlled airspace, it is still highly advisable to be in contact with the aerodrome's approach/radar frequency when operating in such close proximity. By being in communication with the controller, it demonstrates good airmanship and further reassures the controller you are aware of their airspace and that you are not likely to ignorantly infringe upon it.

The control area's airspace is structured in such a way to manage the flow of traffic in and out of the Aerodrome Traffic Zone (ATZ), usually along the extended centreline of the airfield's main runway. The ATZ is controlled by the tower and is represented in the above diagrams as the small, circular block of airspace in the centre, between the surface and 2,000 feet. The ATZ's jurisdiction will vary in diameter depending on the length of the aerodrome's longest runway; the different classifications and dimensions of aerodrome's ATZ can be found in *The Air Pilot's*

Manual 2: Air Law & Meteorology and are particularly useful to know. Aircraft climbing and descending within the extended envelopes of airspace outside of the ATZ are managed by an approach, departure or radar controller on a different frequency to that of the tower.

M ost aircraft that are employed for the purpose of flight training are equipped with some basic form of navigational equipment. However, as a student private pilot, your exposure to this equipment will be limited, as for all intents and purposes you are being trained to be a visual pilot.

Navigation has come on a long way since the advent of powered flight in 1903. At this point in history, navigation was a term only associated with the sea. Historically, before the introduction of satellite positioning, ships would navigate by taking fixes of the stars using a sextant and reference them to the Nautical Almanac publication in order to chart their position. On a cloudless night at sea, this method was particularly accurate owing to the slow movement of the ship and the near-zero light pollution, which gave way for minimal light refraction when measuring a star's position. However, in aviation, this method is not as applicable. An aircraft's speed is notably higher than a ship, meaning that by the time a calculation of position is made, it would be largely out-of-date. Furthermore, when operating over ground, sight taking of stars would be increasingly difficult with the light pollution from cities and built-up populations. These two variables combined would make a position fix difficult to calculate accurately. This meant that in the preliminary years of aviation, navigation was limited to visual and line-of-sight means. As such, the first commercial service, which was between Tampa and St. Petersburg in Florida, was a mere 23-minute flight operated at 15 feet by a boat plane across the bay. However, this service alone greatly reduced the transit time between the two cities, which before relied on lengthy railroad journeys. Such a reduction in journey time laid the foundation for more commercial and practical expectations from aircraft.

Aerial navigation was limited to visual references for much of the first half of the 20th century. As aircraft performance and endurance improved, there was a requirement for the advance of efficient navigation. The longer journeys of the 1910s and 1920s were executed by following coastlines or existing railway lines that dominated and mapped out the industrial age in both the USA and Europe. These tracks often resulted in unwanted, but unavoidable, additional mileages and longer journey times. With an understanding how wind affected aircraft, in terms of drift and groundspeed, some direct, longer journeys were attempted. With a wind vector, an indicated airspeed, a distance and a course, early pioneers could calculate a course to steer and calculate a time of arrival – a skill taught in the PPL syllabus! However, the result of travelling 300 miles on a single heading, with a wind component that would invariably change, and over a featureless terrain, meant that many of these flights missed their intended destination upwards of 50 miles. There were very few accurate visual charts that covered a wide area for the purpose of aerial navigation. In the UK, for example, many of the available charts and maps were produced by Ordnance Survey. However, scales available were large – in the region of 1:2,500 and 1:10,000. Whilst incredibly detailed, for longer journeys pilots would need multiple maps and, given their speed, would likely transit through the area of coverage quite punctually, resulting in a lot of cluttering and moving of maps.

By the early 1920s, aircraft were being used to ferry mail across the USA from coast-to-coast, but only in daylight. An aircraft would be loaded with the mail and flown until nightfall when, thereafter, it would be loaded onto a train. This process took two business days. Aircraft would not fly during the night because of the inability to accurately navigate vast areas of featureless terrain in the central and mid-west plains of the USA. By 1925, this challenge was overcome by the installation of 284 light beacons over 2,665 miles of land from San Francisco to New York – roughly one every 10 miles. This dramatically cut down the service from 48 hours to 33 hours and was achieved with the use of seven aircraft operating in a relay operation. This concept paved the way for the 24-hour operation of aircraft; however, it was limited in its scope. Aircraft had to follow a fixed route, meaning en-route weather could pose a risk to navigation if there were a need to divert from the route, and the roll-out of additional light beacons for further routes would be costly. A solution was needed to allow aircraft to navigate between a network of points, and to be able to do so accurately, without the need for visual contact in the case where visibility was poor.

The solution was found during the late 1920s and early 1930s through the implementation of radio. A popular consumer entertainment commodity at the time, it also had its commercial and navigational qualities. An aircraft would be fitted with a directional antenna and tune to the frequency of a radio station. An instrument in the cockpit would relay the received data into a directional display giving the track from the station – the range, however, would be unknown. The crew would then tune into a second station and plot the track from that station, also. Both tracks, at the point where they intersect, would produce a position fix for the aircraft. Furthermore, with the use of radio, it also meant that, theoretically, the transcontinental light system could be replaced with radio beacons. An aircraft could track the source of the radio waves with its antenna and, once overhead, could tune to the next beacon on its route, and so on and so forth, without the need for good visibility. But that, too, had its drawbacks. The antenna would only show the heading to the station and would not be able to account for drift. Essentially meaning that the pilot would invariably be 'chasing the needle' to the station. Of course, as the aircraft approaches the radio station, the signals become stronger and the instrument would become more sensitive, leading the pilot to make more adjustments. This is demonstrated in the graphic below.

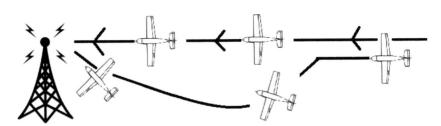

Note that the aircraft in the lower section of the image is experiencing drift as a result of an unknown wind component; however, the nose of the aircraft remains pointed to the radio station at all times. In this instance, the pilot has followed the needle by keeping the radio station in direct sight of their antenna. By doing so, they have flown additional mileage and burnt additional fuel. This phenomenon is very similar to that described in chapter 26 when trying to arrive overhead a landmark with a wind component – the only difference being that in this scenario the aircraft is tracking a signal not a visual landmark.

What will be covered in the PPL will be the tracking and use of a VOR (VHF Omnidirectional Range station). Without going too far into the technical elements of the VOR, as this is best taught by an instructor, I would strongly advise reading up on VORs and how they are of use to a PPL pilot. If you have commercial ambitions, having a foundation in this topic will aid your future training. VORs are regarded as more fundamental in commercial and advanced instrument flying; however, they have a place and function within private flying also. One tip I was shown, which I feel is important to share, is how a VOR can be used to avoid airspace.

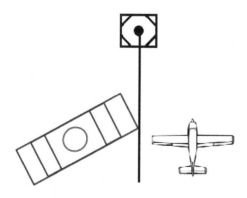

On your chart, a line can be drawn from a VOR to the furthest most protruding point of the control zone's airspace you are looking to avoid. In this example, if you stray to the left of that radial, it will be displayed visually on the VOR instrument and you will know that you will eventually impede on airspace. However, if you remain to the right of the radial, as depicted, you will remain clear. This is, I feel, an essential technique and one of the most important skills to take away from your training.

This brief on radio navigation and its purpose, I hope, will provide a solid groundwork and introduction to what radio navigation is and why and how we use it.

T his chapter, I suppose, is one that a good proportion of students may be able to relate to – particularly those who have commercial ambitions or those who, by nature, are quite self-critical. This topic is one that I was only able to fully comprehend once I had discussed it with my friends and family, and only after I had gained my licence. It is a psychological phenomenon called impostor syndrome. Loosely, it is the pattern of thought whereby an individual doubts their own achievements and holds the fear of being exposed as a fraud despite evidence suggesting otherwise and in favour of their accomplishments. Individuals experiencing impostor syndrome put their success down to luck and the phenomenon can leave the individual feeling anxious and out of place.

In relation to flight training, there are several factors that I feel can induce the onset of impostor syndrome. The first is being surrounded by highly accomplished and qualified instructors whose skills and, perhaps, in some circumstances, lifestyle you wish to emulate. Having this awareness, coupled with receiving positive feedback complimenting your flying, can, counterintuitively, lead to feelings of doubt. Having an experienced instructor say you flew well, or that your landing was better than what they could have produced, can deliver quite the opposite result than what was truthfully intended. If you are a self-critical person, you might judge their feedback as unfounded, or feel their comments are intended to pacify you. In fact, you may very well have produced a very good landing and are worthy of the praise. Of course, thoughts like this are erratic in nature, and whilst you may have performed a great landing, impostor syndrome can shepherd you into thinking it was a fluke or pure luck and had no basis in skill, co-ordination or knowledge.

Secondly, the community, whilst very welcoming, can unintentionally be quite polarising; especially so, if you are trying to complete your licence on a budget. Undoubtedly, you will meet many hobby pilots along the way who will relish the opportunity to tell you of their flying adventures; of how they flew their family 300 miles away on a long weekend on the continent in their privately owned aircraft. I am sure their intention will not be to make you feel jealous, but rather to share their interest with a likeminded individual. However, it may lead you to question how these people are able to afford extravagant fly-outs and have you mulling over whether or not you can really afford to maintain this hobby. I recall being stood at a bar with three other pilots, all of whom were talking rather casually about their flying exploits – journeys overseas, long flights in big, more powerful aircraft than I trained in – all sounding very costly. Although I had many valuable and relevant things to add to that conversation, I felt put off from inputting and stood there feeling like a bit of an impostor.

This was largely because I felt as though I could not match with them on a financial level, which, in hindsight, is ridiculous as the discussion had nothing to do with money. Details about their aircraft, where they were flying and how long they flew for were only ever intended to provide context to their story. The impostor phenomenon made me misconstrue elements of the conversation in a way that made me feel isolated.

As an advanced warning, even when you complete your licence you may experience these kinds of feelings. Even on the day of my test, I was concerned that I was not qualified to even be in the presence of an examiner despite completing all the necessary criteria. Even when I was told that I passed, I still felt that I had managed to cheat and deceive my way through the syllabus and that I had defrauded the system. It is a very odd feeling but I am sure it is something many can relate to. I have held my licence for some time now and I still, occasionally, have these random episodes whereby I feel I have not achieved reaching this goal. As you can imagine, it is rather underwhelming when you consider the amount of effort and sacrifice that goes into completing flight training. I suppose, in those instances, you just move on to tackle the next challenge that life produces.

Perhaps, you may think this chapter may not apply to you, but I am sure, in some manifestation or another, there are themes discussed in this chapter that will be relatable, however subtle they may be.

One of the more humorous things you will learn to appreciate, as your aviation knowledge and flying skills develop, is how little the general public know about aviation. The many faux pas you will begin to notice committed by the blissfully ignorant public or commentators will keep you entertained, but equally dismayed! Here is an example of one I came across recently on a 24-hour news site. It was a picture taken down the centreline of a runway – on it was a large commercial airliner approaching the camera, clearly two-thirds down the runway with a very nose-high attitude. The caption read 'A British Airways jet landing on the runway' – however, it was clearly taking off. If the aircraft was landing that far down the runway, with that high a nose attitude and with minimal flap, then that is a really undesirable situation to be in and I would not want to be where the camera was standing!

Flying, as a whole, is not a topic the masses overly understand, hence the reason why so many people have a fear of flying. But what is less understood is the service that air traffic controllers provide. Your average person on the street may know that an air traffic controller clears aircraft to land and take-off and directs planes around the sky, but, of course, as pilots we know there this a lot more to their role – or at least we should. Still, many pilots are ignorant to air traffic controllers' work outside of the services they regularly request of them. Your communication over the radio is almost scripted, and in the earlier stages of your training you keep your fingers crossed that the air traffic controller does not deviate from the script you are anticipating in return! On a 'good' day, you deliver your pre-prepared lines, you may request a basic service, and you are met with the expected replies and you can focus on flying the aircraft within the envelope you are comfortable. When this is the case, everything runs smoothly and your interaction with air traffic control is procedural and your communication is limited to the bare-essential minimums. This is the ideal situation and the state of operation that air traffic control like to maintain and deliver to pilots operating within their airspace.

Air traffic controllers do, however, offer a number of different services to a number of different aircraft simultaneously. Your service request may be one of a dozen services that an air traffic controller is handling at once. These include services to both instrument flight rule (IFR) and visual flight rules (VFR) traffic – each of which operates to different procedures and minima. Where possible, to aid your situational awareness and airmanship, try and arrange a visit to a tower or speak with an air traffic controller. There are many useful and interactive videos available online that can provide a sense of the work they undertake; however, having the opportunity to ask questions of an air traffic controller is invaluable, and I would recommend you seek out such an opportunity. They will be able to provide a context and insight into their individual work that will help you appreciate their purpose. Surprisingly, many pilots have a fear of upsetting air traffic controllers by becoming flustered and failing to read back correctly. Ultimately, their goal is to provide a safe, coherent and concise service to maintain separation, and that is their justification in seeking out a fully clear and understood read-back.

If your training is at a small, controlled airfield then you may be able to arrange a visit at a quieter time. Quite possibly, as part of a small group – this should not be too difficult to organise through your club who are likely to have a sound working relationship with the control tower. At an uncontrolled field, you are likely to find a radio operator at peak times or a flight information service officer (FISO) who may also be able to provide some information to you. These personnel may be more accessible than in a secure tower operation, though their control and jurisdiction is far more restricted than the remit of an air traffic control officer. At large airfields, for example at international airports, an air traffic controller's role will be more of a pure function, controlling traffic in and out of the ATZ. However, at smaller fields they are likely to have additional responsibilities to manage such as weather observation and aircraft stand allocations. At larger airfields these functions would be separate roles in themselves allocated to an airfield operations team or an air traffic control assistant.

You will be surprised to learn that the control tower does not solely deal with aircraft alone. They also liaise with the wider communities in relation to drone operation, firework and laser displays, and other aerial operations that may pose a risk or obstruction to the safe and orderly progress of aircraft through their area of control.

If you are not in a position to visit the tower at the field at which you train, then this would be the perfect opportunity to visit a different airfield and observe their operation. The type of airfield, whether it is controlled or uncontrolled, has an overwhelming influence on how the airfield operates. For example, at larger, controlled airfields you can expect to find a greater level of security and restrictions to airside access. However, at an uncontrolled aerodrome you will likely be able to easily access the aircraft and the runway with minimal restriction, besides a sign that may read 'Pilots only beyond this point'. A key difference between the larger airfields and their smaller counterparts are the services available on the airfield. Larger airfields, normally with a commercial operation, will have emergency teams to include fire and medical response, and also a robust emergency response plan. Resources at smaller, uncontrolled aerodromes are likely to be sparser. As a point of good airmanship, it would be sensible to read an aerodrome's operations manual ahead of your arrival/ departure. Most aerodromes will have this online on their website or, alternatively, it could probably be emailed in advance; I choose to be in contact with the airfield team at least a week or so ahead of my proposed visit. The operations manual will include emergency response procedures amongst other information, such as joining procedures, available services such as catering, hours of operations etc.

briefly mentioned in the previous chapter the work air traffic control undertakes with regards to drones and other aerial hazards. There are numerous hazards, not just aerial hazards, that pose a risk to the safe passage of an aircraft, and as such a savvy pilot should be aware of these to minimise the likelihood of an accident.

It may sound unlikely at first, but airfields are actually a haven for wildlife –particularly birds and small mammals. An airfield typically includes a relatively protected large and open swathe of land, which is an ideal environment for smaller animals to thrive; as such, airfields act as micro habitats for these animals away from the wider environment, which typically offer threats. Unfortunately, however, now and then aircraft and animals do come into conflict on the ground and, more worryingly, in the air. It is not uncommon to come into contact with a small mammal, such as a hare, whilst taxiing – often you will see them scattering and scurrying for shelter into long grass as you taxi near them. Once aligned on the runway, ready for departure, be sure to have a good look across and down the runway and be prepared to delay your departure in the case of wildlife on the runway. If you do spot any wildlife, make a report over the radio to the controller who may be able to dispatch a vehicle to clear the wildlife from the runway. At an uncontrolled airfield without a radio operator, making an open-call is in the name of good airmanship in order to share this information with other aircraft operators. Never rest on the ill-informed assumption that the wildlife will naturally scatter once you throttle up and steam towards it – startled wildlife can behave in an unpredictable nature. An animal, like a deer, for example, may very well freeze and hold its position if startled. A sensible mind would deduce that it is not a risk worth taking. A quick internet search along the lines of 'plane vs deer' will produce several results detailing the damage in the aftermath of such a collision.

Airborne wildlife, i.e. birds, are a larger prevailing threat to aviation. Bird strikes are most common during take-off and landing, at altitudes where the vast majority of birds fly. A study by the University of Nebraska found that out of a total of 38,961 reported bird strikes in the United States between 1990-2004, 28,806 strikes occurred below 500 feet*. These were largely contacts with gulls, perching birds and predatory birds, such as hawks. Above 500 feet, the most common bird families that aircraft encountered were geese, ducks and other waterfowl. The threat of a bird strike is particularly difficult to avoid and we,

---

* Height Distribution of Birds Recorded by Collisions with Civil Aircrafthttp://digitalcommons.unl.edu/cgi/viewcontent. cgi?article=1496&context=icwdm_usdanwrc

as pilots, must be vigilant and alert to the warning signs of bird presence. Particularly, this includes flying at dawn and dusk, during migratory periods and operating in the vicinity of bird sanctuaries and conservation areas. Having this knowledge and awareness will go far in mitigating the likelihood of an encounter. In the event of an impending bird strike, it is very unlikely you that you will be able to spot the hazard before any contact, the likelihood being that you will not be aware of a collision until it is over. This is why prevention is the best cure in these instances.

Further to birds, drones are now also becoming an ever-growing risk to aircraft in flight. Drone activity is on the increase, with many consumer-level drones becoming inexpensive commodities. As a consumer, you or I could purchase a drone today and have it operating from our doorstep the next day. So accessible and novel have drones become that consumers are often unaware of the threat they pose and, indeed, their responsibilities as an operator. Many consumers will ignorantly launch a drone above their heads with little awareness of the disruption and damage they could cause. Often operators will self-certify their operation as safe with little regard for the rules and laws governing the operation of drones – either through ignorance or a lack of caring. To avoid naming and shaming, or giving the particular uploader the publicity, there is a video on YouTube showing footage taken from a drone overhead a large built-up city on the southcoast of England. In the video, the user annotates their footage with rather incriminating commentary, stating they are operating at 200m (660 feet) – which exceeds the UK's current limit of 122m (400 feet). In addition to the height violation, the camera pans around to an international airport less than 3,000m away. The distance at which a drone can operate from an airport has since been (controversially) relaxed to 1,000m, but at the time of uploading the person was openly violating two rules that safeguard aircraft operating within the jurisdiction of the airport's control zone. The position of the drone in the video falls within the circuit and approach profile of the main runway, which is highly concerning.

In the UK, drones can operate within a kilometre of an airport's boundary and up to 400 feet. However, these lax restrictions are under review in the UK following disruptions at Gatwick and Heathrow airports, which were potentially caused by criminal drone activity. In Germany, this is slightly more restrictive at 1,500 metres in range and 164 feet in altitude within controlled airspace. In French law, if the airfield's runway is less than 1,200 metres and not equipped with instrument approach installations, a drone may not operate within 5,000 metres of the end of the runway and 500 metres from the edge. Whilst restrictions are in place and enforced, where applicable, the onus falls solely on the operator to use their drone safely and within the law. The concerning factor is that many operators are unaware of their responsibility, duty and obligation to operate in a safe and legal way. The drone market is growing; this needs to be supplemented with greater co-operation and communication between the drone and aviation communities. That said, the average consumer who purchases a drone just wants to unpack their latest gadget and launch it – getting them to first learn the rules of the air is a daunting challenge. Without tighter regulation and proficiency testing, I cannot see this being achieved. This will certainly be a topic to monitor in the coming years.

A further hazard to be cautious of during flight is a laser attack. Unfortunately, there are irresponsible individuals in the community who threaten the safety of aircraft and their occupants by focusing a high-intensity laser at the cockpit in an effort to distract, disable and disorientate the aircrew. Laser attacks, when they occur, are mainly prevalent during the take-off and landing phases of flight, which are, typically, the times where workload is at its peak. A distraction by a laser can lead to workload saturation which, in turn, could cause potentially severe mistakes being made at this critical stage. Equally, a laser attack can result in damage to the eyes. Laser attacks can also occur during daytime and at altitude, such is the intensity of hand-held lasers. In the event of a laser attack, a pilot should remain calm and focussed, maintain the trinity of aviate, navigate and communicate, in that order. If it means breaking off an approach to turn away from the laser, then do so. Establish your position and then make a report over the radio to draw attention to the attacks. The radio operator will then make a report to the police. To further develop the data on laser attacks and support the community, you should file an aviation safety report to your governing aviation authority.

The last hazard I want to touch upon in this chapter is not a physical obstruction or interference by an external faction. It is, in fact, the risk we pose to ourselves. We, as pilots, have a duty and responsibility to ensure we are fit for flight. This does not just encapsulate the obvious – we would, of course, never fly intoxicated, or otherwise. It also encompasses less obvious factors that as pilots we need to actively consider. Are we well rested? Are we physically able? Does your bruised elbow affect your ability to control the aircraft? Are you well hydrated and alert? These factors we bear little attention to elsewhere in life. Countless times I've driven to work tired, dehydrated and harbouring an injury. But why should it be any different? In an ideal world it should not be. However, on the most part, those of us who can drive do most days and have developed a high level of proficiency and muscle memory in relation to the task. Moreover, the task of driving itself is less demanding than flight. Driving has become a routine task in many of our lives. That is not to say we are less focussed or less fit to drive because of this; the point is our repetition and proficiency means our brains require less active concentration in order to complete the task. I would imagine the same would apply to flying if we were all able to afford to fly 10 hours a week, which is roughly the average amount of time an individual spends driving in a seven-day period

R everting back to topics more pertinent to your training, as you progress through your navigation exercises you will note an increase in the amount of paperwork and equipment you will be carrying. A training aircraft tends not to be overly spacious and, as a result of carrying a lot of equipment, the cockpit can become quite cramped and cluttered. Despite having little space in which to store your belongings, it becomes notoriously difficult to locate things when you need them. Having a flight bag does help with the general transportation of your belongings, but in the air the last thing you want to be doing is rummaging through your bag, that is stored in the rear of the aircraft, looking for your diversion ruler. The stress of not being able to find something you are looking for, coupled with constantly looking in the back of aircraft, can lead to distraction, a loss of concentration and may, invariably, lead to disorientation and motion sickness.

There are multiple techniques and processes you can go through to effectively reduce the levels of clutter in the aircraft and on your lap. The first piece of advice I would give is to review your kneeboard before each flight and discard any old, irrelevant paperwork kept in, or on it. There is no logic in taking to the sky with a scrap piece of paper with notes and weather information from two weeks ago. It will only serve to cause confusion as you quote the wrong 'information' and will, ultimately, lead to frustration as you look for space to jot down more recent information. Of course, you will then lose that information in amongst all your previous scribblings. Good practice would be to replenish your kneeboard with fresh paper before each flight or, alternatively, a new pilot log sheet, with space to record off/on blocks times and ATIS information. Having a fresh layout before you sets the right tone for your flight.

Secondly, I would advise having a small arsenal of pens available to you – to include a spare semi-permanent pen to annotate your VFR chart with. On my mock test, I dropped my sole semi-permanent marker under my seat, so I had to revert to drawing on my chart with a biro instead – very undesirable. Having these pens easily accessible and close to hand is equally as important. Pens stored in your jeans pocket will be hard to get to. With space at a premium, you will struggle greatly to wrestle a pen free from your trousers with your pride intact. Ideally, you want a shirt with a pocket or, perhaps, a NATO style jumper, during colder weather, with a pen sleeve on the arm for a quick and dignified retrieve.

On your lap, you are likely to have your kneeboard, a VFR chart and your checklist. Unfortunately, there is not a great deal you can do in reducing or limiting the presence of your chart besides storing it down the side of your chair when it is not needed. Your checklist, however, can be reworked to make it more cockpit friendly and ergonomic. This is a tip I learned from a friend: rather than having to contend with a flimsy flip chart, which can occasionally be difficult to navigate through, find the time to type up your checklist and print it onto a two-sided A4 sheet and laminate it. This made referencing my checklist a slicker process and reduced the time that I would otherwise be spending searching and flipping through my old flip chart. Having it laminated also allowed me to annotate it with a semi-permanent marker, which helped in learning and becoming more fluid with the checklist procedures. Revisiting your VFR chart briefly, there is a way in which the chart can be folded that can effectively render the chart with a second use as a bag. If the chart is first folded in half and then folded in the Z-fold (or concertina) format, within the folds of the chart a small pocket will created – ideal for storing your flight computer, diversion and checklist.

A final point, which should really go without saying, is the need to only take equipment that is absolutely necessary for the task of flying out to the aircraft. If only flying locally, is there really a need to bring along your large flight bag with your *Air Pilot Manual* books enclosed? If you are training in the circuit, is it necessary to bring your large ruler and your flight computer? Most likely not. Also, only aim to bring equipment that is easily stowed and accessible, such as items that can be secured neatly in your kneeboard.

A s you gain further independence in your training, through the way of solo flights and navigation planning, give some thought to what kind of future in flying you want once you gain your PPL. All the while you are in training, there is a set and pre-determined syllabus in place to develop your skills and build your hours. However, once you gain your PPL that mentoring and guidance can effectively stop and you are left to your own devices to decide what your next steps are.

I have met numerous pilots who have let their skills and proficiency drop off through lack of confidence and they end up remaining in the circuit or local area for hours after the issue of the PPL. Yes, there are those pilots who are happy to hold their PPL and just fly locally around their airfield, and that is completely fine! But there are some pilots who lack the confidence to take their flying further. If you identify with this, once qualified, I would advise speaking to the flying school you trained with. For the same training rate that you paid while under tuition, you will be able to book an instructor to come fly with you. You will not be under instruction per se, but you will have an experienced set of hands on standby to settle nerves, instil confidence and offer some form of input.

In the more preferred and positive outcome, your future flying plans are vast! Back to the present, it could be the case that your flying goals have changed now that you are further through the syllabus and can conceptualise what the final product will be like. This can also be further influenced by your wider networking with other pilots or through discovery of new airfields etc. In essence, there are a number of factors that can have a bearing on your goals. But what is important to note, is that your goals will continually evolve as you develop more experience. These goals do not exclusively have to be in relation to gaining a particular skill or rating to add to your licence, they could be targets; for example, flying 20 hours this year, or visiting a different country. It is important to set goals in order to challenge yourself, but also to keep your flying exciting. During the navigation element of the syllabus, I took to the internet to discover airfields within an hour of my club. I had planned my route to an airfield on the south coast of England months before I had even passed my skills test, and I was pleased to make that trip my first flight once my licence came through. That trip then inspired me to look a little further. So you can see, having goals serve as a motivator to enhance your flying experience.

Once you have gained your PPL, you can look to add additional ratings to your licence to qualify you to fly in more diverse conditions. As such, many pilots choose to undertake the Night Rating. The Night Rating includes five hours of flying (a mix of dual and solo) and around five hours of theoretical tuition. This short course usually costs, on average, £1,000 (1,100 €*). Whilst flying at night has its challenges, many choose to undertake the training to primarily extend their accessibility to flying; particularly during the winter months when sunset can be as early as 1600.

The same can be said for the Instrument Rating (Restricted) or IR(R), which in some European nations maybe referred to as the En-route Instrument Rating. As the name suggest, this rating allows you to fly on instruments enroute in the event that you may encounter cloud of poor visibility. However, weather conditions at the arrival and departure stations must be within VFR limits. In the UK, the privileges of the IR(R) can only be exercised within UK airspace. To fly internationally in Europe in marginal conditions, a full, unrestricted, Instrument Rating is required. Much like the night rating, the IR(R) qualification vastly increases a pilot's access to flying during periods of the year when the weather would otherwise not be suitable for flying. In the UK, the course includes 15 hours of dual flying, a theoretical exam and a skills test.

If you have plans to eventually go commercial, training for both of these ratings is highly advisable. In order to undertake commercial training you are only required to already hold the Night Rating. However, additionally having the IR(R) means you are able to apply for a 10-hour concession when undertaking the full IR later during commercial training. Not only will these ratings have you in a favourable position at the start of your training, they will also help in building your hours more swiftly as you will not be purely restricted to operate in fair conditions during daylight.

---

*   Exchange rate £1 = 1.10 € (Winter 2018)

n the previous chapter, some thought was given to your post-training options with the goal of developing advanced flying skills. However, in the here and now, I want to draw some thought to another skill that needs to be given some consideration. All too often in this book I have mentioned the disadvantages of familiarity and how it can catch us out when we find ourselves in an environment that differs from the norm. However, it is the familiarity of our instructor, our airfield, our club etc that provides the foundation for us, as pilots, to build on our experience. In particular, I want to draw attention to the familiarity you have developed with the aircraft you train on.

If you train at a small club, you may have flown only a single aircraft. By this I do not mean a single type, I mean a single registration. Quite possibly, at a larger club, you may have trained on several aircraft; all the same type, but different registrations. Despite being the same type, you can, perhaps, agree with me that there are subtle differences and characteristics that make each aircraft very individual. You could argue they are all the same aircraft, just different registrations. To some extent – yes, that is true. I can concede that when these aircraft rolled off the production line it is very likely there were minimal differences between them – that is only true, of course, if they are all the same variant. However, over a period of time, aircraft undergo various maintenance and repairs, upgrades and restorations that have an overall impact on their handling and characteristics. As most of the aircraft used for flight training are over 30 years old, it is likely they are a very different aircraft now than they were when they first entered service. If you can relate this to driving – if two identical cars came off the production line at the same time and, five years later, you were to see the same two cars again, you would notice differences in their appearance and performance. Factors such as their drivers and their environment will have major influences on their characteristics. With some experience, I can now appreciate the comments other pilots make when they say, 'AB, that is a good aircraft'. Whilst the PPL syllabus teaches you how to fly, I feel the training is better defined as teaching you how to fly the aircraft you train on. I am comfortable flying the two aircraft I trained on during my training. I would not, however, feel comfortable or qualified to be able to climb into any other aircraft and operate it.

Some of these characteristics you will begin to have an appreciation for each time you go flying. Perhaps already you have had a moment where your club tells you you are flying a certain registration and you immediately think, 'that is the aircraft with the stiff primer' or 'that is the aircraft that will not start on the first ignition'. All these observations will make you more familiar with the aircraft and make you more in-sync with its performance.

I learned to fly on two aircraft, both had their interesting nuances. One aircraft had a tendency to pull to the right in the cruise, whilst the other would induce interference into the headset when the electric motor-driven flaps were retracted, causing an awful crackle to ring through the headset. The latter would always happen as my instructor and I were taxiing past the airfield tower, which led us to believe it was caused by our proximity to their communication systems. It was only when we taxied past after a flapless landing that I realised the noise was not there on that occasion. We determined it had nothing to do with the proximity to the tower; it was, in fact, just co-incidence that every time we had taxied past the tower previously, we were usually in the process of deploying or retracting our flap setting. We tested the flaps again whilst in the air, and, as expected, the same noise persisted. We had uncovered a minor electrical wiring issue!

The aircraft you train on, whether it is just a single registration or three different aircraft, will have an interesting history to them. You will feel better connected with the aircraft if you were to undertake some research on its previous flying history. Your club should be able to tell you a little more about where it has come from – their previous owner at least. I found simply searching the aircraft's registration through an internet search engine would bring up photographs and some minor history. It can also be of interest to see where the aircraft has flown to, as many aircraft spotters will share their photographs of the aircraft online. I was surprised to find one of the aircraft I trained on had flown to Menorca in the Mediterranean. Through aircraft databases found online, you may be able to find if the aircraft operated under different registrations in its previous life, which may also open up and lead to different lines of enquiry.

Besides the individual registration history and performance, it is of good airmanship to know information about the type itself. Eventually, when you fly with family and friends as passengers, they are bound to ask for a little bit of information about the aircraft they are flying in. Passengers may be interested in the length and wing span of the aircraft, amongst other trivia like the engine size and capacity. Knowing this information confidently will ease your passengers' nerves and reassure them that the aircraft they are flying in is not just a collection of aluminium sheet and bolts, but that it comes from a lineage of good design and capability.

I can appreciate if this chapter seems somewhat novel, but I firmly attest that having a better understanding and relationship with your aircraft will benefit your performance and your vested interest in flying. It will also be indicative of your knowledge as a pilot when it comes to your skills test, if you can explain minor differences and/or departures from your checklist on the basis of the aircraft flown.

The qualifying cross-country flight is the middle of three key milestones in flight training; with the earlier being your first solo, and the latter being your skills test. Between your first solo and your cross-country flight, you will spend around 20 hours practising circuits, practised forced landings, steep turns, stalling and several dual and solo navigation routes that begin and depart at your operating base. A secondary goal of these hours is to hone your confidence, proficiency and independence in making decisions. The premise of this chapter is to assess your preparedness for your fast-approaching, qualifying cross-country flight.

As part of the dual navigation exercises, you should expect to be diverted to a nearby alternate airfield; perhaps, simulating a medical emergency or an airfield closure. If the airfield from which you fly is geographically isolated and there are no feasible diversion destinations available, you may be asked to divert to an alternative such as a town or a particular landmark. The objective of the diversion, at this stage at least, is not to judge your arrival procedure or landing, but instead to see how you go about plotting your route there. Your instructor will want to see you establish your position, plot a track, provide a course to steer and generate an accurate ETA based on wind conditions. Expect some leniency with the ETA as your calculations will be based on out-of-date wind data – the wind may very well change. Ultimately, as I am sure you will determine as you progress, your level of safety is the key aspect of your flying that your instructor, and, ultimately, the examiner want to see. If you can demonstrate a diversion that avoids infringing airspace, gets you to the destination promptly and does not threaten the security of yourself or any other air users, you are on the path to success. The diversion was a part of the syllabus I fretted about for a long time. In the end, it is actually a controlled exercise in which you have the opportunity to display some autonomy and executive decision making; in my case, my instructor feigned to be incapacitated and would not respond to me after they proclaimed,'I feel ill, I think we should divert'. A good student should be prepared for this element of the syllabus. I was given a subtle hint quite a away in advance during my navigation brief, which I picked up on. I can imagine the stress it would put a student under if they were not anticipating this challenge of their reactions. Though, that said, I suppose that is the nature of diversions – they are often unexpected and not anticipated. But in a training environment, I cannot see any harm in being braced for such an event.

Unless the airfield you fly from is not suitable for flying circuits, it is unlikely you would have visited another aerodrome by air. As a further learning point beyond your diversion calculations, take your arrival into the diversion airfield as your first introduction to visiting a new one. If your instructor had previously 'taken ill', they will almost certainly experience a miraculous recovery and offer guidance as you make your approach. I would, however, caution you not to be overly harsh on your performance as it is likely your arrival and joining procedure will be a bit untidy. Your previous circuit and landing work would have largely taken place at your home airfield, so being introduced to a new environment can be perplexing. A good landing will usually follow a good circuit and approach; however, at a new airfield, your visual cues and reference points for your circuit are likely to be unknown at this point. This will likely be the first occasion where you will really need to judge your circuit by eye. This can be a challenge, but your instructor will be on-hand to guide you through the joining procedure. After all, they are likely to have visited this airfield a number of times before. But this arrival into a new airfield will really highlight how familiar and comfortable you are with the territory of your home airfield and how ill-prepared you are for visiting a new one.

So, what is the missing link? Simply, it is the procedure that requires following when arriving at a new airfield. From the skills you have been taught throughout the syllabus, you will have all the components to successfully take-off, navigate enroute and, finally, land. However, venturing into a new aerodrome can be intimidating and our performance can quickly deteriorate in new surroundings. If we are able to brief ourselves before arriving then this could, perhaps, lessen the workload and stress when making our arrival. Thankfully, there is a publication on hand that is available to pilots to consult on such matters. This publication is the Aeronautical Information Service (AIS) and member states of ICAO have an obligation under Annex 15 to provide such a service to air users. A state's AIS is a support system that is built up of three categories. The first is a general section (GEN), which includes recommended practices, abbreviations and lists of services available to pilots. Part 2 is the en-route section (ENR) to include information pertaining to navigation, en-route charts, radio navigation systems and airspace. Lastly, there is the aerodrome section (AD) – it is within this section that both graphical and textual data for airfields can be accessed. All ICAO member states will have an AIS; all of which will provide similar information relevant to that member state's civil aviation operation.

It is definitely worth becoming familiar with your country's AIS publication, and it can be retrieved by a simple internet search. Even if the vast expanse of documentation and information means very little to you at this stage, at least have a browse through its sections to familiarise yourself with its layout. Quite possibly, while navigating through it, you may find familiar documents or a publication/notice that may advance your knowledge and overall airmanship. You could say that a country's AIS is much like an operation manual for their civil aviation operation. As such, it is an invaluable educational tool.

For your first introduction to the AIS, it may be pragmatic to visit the aerodrome (AD) section. If you do not know what your qualifying cross-country route is, then now would be a good time to find out from your club. The club I trained at had one fixed qualifying cross-country route; however, yours may have several.

Once you know the airfields you are set to visit, have a look at the AD aerodrome diagram and textual data. Included in the aerodrome diagram will be a layout of the runway(s), taxiways, parking and other amenities, such as fuelling stations and where the tower is positioned. A small table will include relevant radio frequencies for the airfield. This information will be supplemented in the textual data document with instructions on how to access these services, any restrictions around the aerodrome and other pertinent information such as operational hours, handling services, runway characteristics and length, and obstacles, to name a handful. The latter categories in the textual data – namely, *the local traffic regulations, noise abatement procedures* and the *flight procedures*– will provide a sound understanding of the airfield's operation. These details will include how to join the circuit and in what direction, what height to join at, areas to avoid for noise abatement and other navigational notices to brief yourself with ahead of your arrival.

With this information, you can effectively plan your arrival and departure. There may be several different joining and departing procedures that may be assigned to you depending on your arrival/departure direction. A trick I have learned is to draw the circuit, or any other instruction provided, onto your kneeboard. Firstly, sketch down the runway's alignment with respect to north. If, say, you were arriving from the east – draw a mock-up representation of your inbound track and then draw the instruction provided. Here is an example overleaf, using an arrival from the east:

'A-BC, join right-hand downwind for runway 03.'

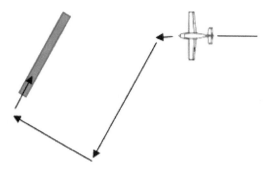

The same principles can be applied when departing.

Having an idea of how you will arrive will greatly assist in your forward planning and will lessen the workload in the cockpit as you approach your destination. A good pilot will call ahead to the arrival station while on the ground to ask what runway is in use and what the circuit pattern is, so this mental picture can be produced before setting off. However, things can and do change so be prepared to think on your feet if the instruction given differs from the plan.

W ithout going into too much detail about how you should prepare your plan for your qualifying cross-country route, I have several reflections and tips to dispense to better prepare you for your first attempt with an instructor. Whilst flying the route solo is the most celebrated and lauded event, I found flying the route for the first time, with an instructor, to be where the real challenge is. You may, at first, think flying the route solo, unaccompanied, will be the real test of your abilities. But bear in mind, before you fly it solo, you would have already flown the route through once before with your instructor, somewhat as a dress rehearsal; so by the time you fly it solo you would have already visited the airfields, dealt with the various procedures and have some foresight into what to expect. Flying the route with your instructor, I feel, is more load-bearing as you have an experienced pilot observing your flying, scrutinising your planning and assessing your execution. After all, you will not be authorised to fly the route solo until you can demonstrate to your instructor you are capable of getting around the route safely.

These are some points to consider and prepare for:

1 – Make sure you arrive on the day with a solid, viable plan. Not just lines drawn on your chart, but also a journey log complete with distances measured, headings, groundspeed and times calculated from the most current weather.

2 – Ensure you have a complete list of all the radio station frequencies you intend to talk to from departure, enroute and arrival. Be sure to write down the aerodromes' ATIS frequencies also, if applicable. If you are visiting a larger, controlled airfield you may have talk to multiple controllers in quick succession. As you near its control zone, you are likely to speak to the approach controller, then, perhaps, the director frequency, before being handled by the tower. At smaller controlled sites, you may speak to a single air traffic controller who manages the approach, tower and ground functions, all at once, on a single frequency. At these larger airfields, you may have up to five frequencies: the ATIS, the approach, the director, the tower and a ground frequency. Have them all to hand, as any combination of them will be in use depending on how busy the operation is. Another big tip is to actually annotate what the frequency is, whether it is the ATIS, approach, tower etc. I flew with a friend once who had written down the airfield name and three frequencies beneath it, thinking they were well prepared and efficient. As

we approached the airfield, I watched them waste time cycling through two wrong frequencies – the approach and tower frequencies – before finally inputting the correct one to hear the ATIS report. Researching and knowing your frequencies will garner the praise of your instructor and will support your case in being sent solo.

3 – Be sure to book in with the relevant airfields. This is mainly to avoid any awkward en-route conversations or possible rejections. Your club will probably know the numbers to call but, equally, you will be able to find the relevant contact details on the airfield's website. Alternatively, this information can be found in the AIS (section 3 – AD) within the textual data for the airfield. While on the phone to them, why not ask what runway is in use – a tip discussed in an earlier chapter – to plan your arrival.

4 – On the day, take a look over your route and check to see if there are any Notices to Airmen (NOTAMs) or airspace restrictions in place that may hinder your progress. Again, refer to your state's AIS, which will list them. However, if you are operating in Europe – for a graphical representation of NOTAMs – I would recommend a site called www.NOTAMinfo.com which has the function to overlay NOTAMs and navigational warnings onto a map. Countries covered by this service include: Austria, Belgium, Germany, France, the Netherlands, Italy, the UK and Spain, to name a

few. Unfortunately, the majority of eastern European countries including the Balkan and Baltic states are not included.

5 – It is easy to draw a straight line between two points on your chart, but be cautious of airspace you intend to pass close by. Furthermore, be aware of the airspace above and below you too. Ensure your planned altitude does not see you penetrate an aerodrome's control zone. If you do pass near, above or below a control zone, have their frequency on standby in the case that you need to divert through their airspace. I learned to fly in the southeast of England, and often I would be operating just below the London Terminal Manoeuvring Area (TMA). I had to be particularly mindful of my altitude because the TMA began at 2,500 feet, and I would often linger slightly below at 2,200 feet. At times, it would be nerve wracking to see an Airbus A330, for example, flying only 1,000 feet above me. I was reassured, however, knowing that they were talking to the Terminal Control Centre and I was talking to my relevant, appropriate controller and that we were being managed and separated accordingly.

6 – Really know your air law and ensure you are comfortable with the rules of the air –in particular, knowledge such as marshalling signals, light signals, taxi hold and stop signs. At controlled airfields, where it may be busier, there is a greater pressure to know

such basic courtesies as who has the right of way and to which direction you should turn and pass another aircraft if taxiing towards a head-on conflict, should the situation ever arise. If there was a single air pilot manual I would recommend you carry with you when visiting a new aerodrome, *The Air Pilot's Manual 2: Air Law & Meteorology*, would be it, purely for its operational procedures and rules content.

7 – Remember to bring your wallet to the aircraft! Around the route, you will need to pay landing fees to the airfields you visit. You do not want the added stress and embarrassment of arriving and presenting yourself to the airfield reception without money to pay for your landing. There will always be a solution – like calling up and paying later that day – but it is just an added inconvenience that is best avoided. It is also polite (and politically wise) to treat your instructor to a cup of coffee and a cake on the way around. This also takes off some of the pressure and adds some enjoyment to your qualifying cross-country flight. Eventually, once the licence is in your hands, you will end up visiting plenty of airfield cafes and restaurants anyway, so you may as well start now!

8 – Lastly, enjoy it! Flying is fun and the qualifying cross-country flight embodies what our flying goals are all about. It is an opportunity during the syllabus to experience what flying really entails past your training.

If you appear to enjoy it and seem relaxed, your instructor will be more inclined to authorise your solo flight. The cross-country flight does not require two to three hours of concentrated focus, there will be plenty of opportunity to leisurely talk to your instructor, take in the scenery and just enjoy flying the aircraft. Your qualifying cross-country flight is likely to be the most time you have spent in the air in one day. Expect to very tired by the end of it!

With regards to flying the route solo – it should not be as taxing now you have fully seen the route with an instructor. The same cannot be said for my good friend James, who on his solo was refused permission from his first destination airfield because of some work-in-progress at the field. Once they were convinced to accept him, he then had to wait an hour and half for the second airfield to open. Once at his second airfield he encountered a technical problem that was remedied by a friendly instructor from a different flying school. All-in-all, it took James five and a half hours to fly the route!

I, deliberately, have little else to offer on your solo qualifying cross-country route. This is an opportunity to make the experience your own.

Off the back of your solo qualifying cross-country flight, by and large you would have mostly completed the EASA PPL syllabus. The minimum 10 solo hours needed to qualify for the PPL will come from solo circuits, steep turns and practised forced landings. The solo navigation routes would have roughly constituted half of your 10 solo hours. You would have completed your minimum 25 hours' dual tuition, also. If, by this stage, your hours are still below the 45 required for the issue of the licence, your remaining hours will be built up through dual and solo revision and a mock test. If you are past the 45-hour threshold then your remaining training will move at a pace to the point where you will then be ready to take the skills test.

However, in amongst this exciting, yet fast moving, time, there are likely to be a couple of other administrative ground tasks to complete. These are, namely, completing the rest of your exams, if you have any outstanding, and completing your oral radiotelephony examination. The latter of the two tends to be the most put-off element of the PPL syllabus and I can understand why. Logically, it can make sense to sit the radiotelephony exam after your qualifying cross-country flight — I will detail this later in this chapter. The other reason for delaying this test is because, often, there is very little insight into what actually happens in your radiotelephony exam. Also, I have also received mix reviews on individual's experiences ranging from it being practically impossible to fail, to the other end of the spectrum whereby I have heard it is stressful, difficult and not at all enjoyable. My examiner dispensed to me that there were no set authority-approved tests to examine students against. As such, so long as key elements of radiotelephony procedure are tested, the approved examiner has relative free scope to test you on any radio-related scenario. For those who are unfamiliar with the structure of the exam, it follows a pre-determined route drawn on a chart. The area and stations could well be fictitious, as they were in my case. You are provided with frequencies (or channel numbers) and you are tasked with cycling through the correct frequencies, all the while making the correct call-and-response transmissions as you progress through the route. There is no time pressure and as most calls are initiated by you, you are able to take your time in preparing whatever information you need to transmit. It is not a fast drill exercise — it is to simulate a real-life flying situation. After all, when in the air, an air traffic controller is not necessarily going to be expecting your call when you join a frequency, so you can take as little or as much time as you need to prepare your call. It is also very highly advisable to do so! Fast and mistake-ridden calls will only serve to slow everybody on frequency down. I appreciate there can be a pressure to not hesitate with the issuing of your calls when there is an examiner opposite you or in the other room. However, they are not there to test your speed – they are there to assess your effective communication skills.

Through general research at the time I was looking to sit my radiotelephony exam, I found that most examiners will offer two types of service:

Option 1 – The test only. If you are well versed and prepared in your radiotelephony skills then this may suit you fine. With this option, you may not be briefed, besides obviously the format of the test, so this choice may daunt you as the candidate. On the whole, the test-only option will cost £60 to £80 (66-88 €*).

Option 2 – A brief, mock test and exam session. This is an option I feel most student pilots will favour. It is slightly more costly and through research I have found prices ranging from £100 to £200 (110-220 €*). The value of this option is that the examiner will brief you for a couple of hours on the elements and topics that are relevant to their test – that is not to say, however, that you should not come prepared! The following mock test will serve to settle your nerves and familiarise you with the layout, format and pace of the examination. This is the option I sided with and I would recommend it to new student pilots.

So, how can you best prepare for such an examination? Well, bizarrely, you will have been revising for it every time you have been flying. So long as, of course, your instructor has been

---

* Exchange rate £1 = 1.10 € (Winter 2018)

keeping your radio communications in-check and correcting non-aviation phraseology and procedure. That is why I would only suggest completing your radiotelephony exam once you have completed your dual and solo qualifying cross-country flight. With these flights completed, you will have experienced, several times, the entire stream of calls a pilot makes from start up, taxi and take-off clearances, en-route calls, approach and landing calls etc. Whilst these experiences will serve to bolster your confidence and proficiency, there may be some radio procedures you have not encountered. You may argue that within 45 hours of flying you may have seen, or heard rather, them all. But we must also consider the relatively small area of airspace in which we learn to fly. I, for one, learned to fly in the southeast of England, and now, as I revisit my VFR chart, I flew no further than 70 miles west and 35 miles north of my airfield. When I open up my VFR chart to cover a wider area, I now appreciate there are a variety of different airspace features and restrictions I never experienced. For example, military zones, areas of intense aerial activity and jet airways. I would never have known how, what and who to communicate with. If we are operating in a smaller and familiar section of airspace we can expect to become more efficient in our communication. However, it is when travelling to new areas and pushing ourselves out of our comfort zones where we need to ensure we are prepared and competent – that is our responsibility as pilots. To that end, I would recommend revisiting documents I previously drew your attention to, way back in Chapter 15. Your aviation authority will have a manual that will detail your nation's radio procedure. At European level, EASA also offer a manual for standardised calls. Again, familiarise yourself with Chapter 15 in relation to this.

Once your examination is complete, your examiner will endorse your PPL application form under the relevant Flight Radiotelephony Operators' Licence (FRTOL) section ready to be sent of the aviation authority once you have passed your skills test.

T his next topic, I briefly acknowledged at the beginning of the previous chapter. Further to getting your radiotelephony oral examination out of the way, and with the qualifying cross-country flight also complete, it would be a good time to sit with your club and check through your log book to see how many hours are left to build, if any, and what skills and techniques require revision.

Your flight club will, of course, have a training record of your progress, but your log book needs to reflect that as both documents will be scrutinised in order to confirm you have the right number of hours and have received the correct amount of training for each exercise. Hence why it is incredibly important to record all the exercises you have trained on in the remarks column of your log book. Ensure there is clarity with your instructor after each flight so that you correctly record the right exercise and that both records match.

It is best to reconcile your log book after your solo qualifying cross-country flight because, once that is complete, you are, effectively, preparing for your test. If you are looking to pass within the 45-hour minimum, then this opportunity to identify gaps in your hours and knowledge is an important one. Your club will not recommend you for the test unless they are sure that all elements of the syllabus have been covered. If the 45-hour minimum is your focus, then do not end up in the unenviable position where failure to monitor your progress through the syllabus results in you missing your goal. What tends to be the case is that when you approach the end of your training, you are likely to undergo a mock test, which will probably be conducted by a different instructor who you may not have flown with. If you pass this mock, you will then undertake your skills test. So if you are aiming to pass in 45 hours, you ideally want to be in the position where you can undertake your mock test at the 43-hour mark. Can you imagine the disappointment you would feel if you were encroaching on the 43-hour mark for your mock, then you were told by your club you still needed to do another couple of hour of stalling, or steep turns, or whatever to even qualify to sit the mock test. This, in consequence, would bust your goal.

To protect your goal, you need to be forthcoming and closely monitoring your progress. It would not be pragmatic to entrust the management of your training solely to your flight school. That is not to say they are incapable of maintaining the oversight of your records! However, having you as a second pair of eyes to monitor and subsequently guide your training will be more cost-effective and will, hopefully, avoid any disappointment. To conquer this, I devised a small spreadsheet to replicate my log book. It took no more than a half hour to set it up and transpose my written log book over onto it. By producing this spreadsheet, I was able to tally up my hours and monitor the hours spent on each exercise to ensure I had fulfilled the syllabus requirement. Even now, post-training, I use the same spreadsheet to tally my hours. It can also be used to run some interesting figures for analysis, if that is your particular interest. I am able to calculate my total number of landings, what time of the day I regularly fly, what are the most common days of the week. Mainly, information that has no operational bearing but still very interesting, nonetheless. Similar eDocuments and applications are available online through many general aviation websites but these may come at a small fee. Some online aviation community website subscriptions may include such an online log book as part of their membership package.

With your log book reviewed and with the required hours and exercises completed, your instructor and club will look to put you forward for your mock test. Much like my notes and thoughts on the qualifying cross-country flight, I will look to provide some guidance points for your mock test but not your actual skills test. Besides, any pilot worth their salt will treat their mock test with the same precedent as the inevitable skills test. Again, as before with the qualifying cross-country flight, your skills test is very much an individual, unique experience and is there for you to own and direct yourself.

With that disclaimer said, if you treat your mock test like you would your skills test there is next to no difference in how you would prepare and the above becomes rather elementary.

What I would first advise you to do is fly with a different instructor altogether for the purpose of your mock test, where possible. Throughout the majority of my training I flew with two instructors. In my earlier days, I was adamant that I wanted to fly with a single instructor in order to best replicate and learn their way of flying.

My approach and reasoning was that if I could closely emulate their style and procedure, I would quickly progress through the syllabus. By and large, that was the case and it certainly paid off, I feel. Flying with a second instructor, however, brought a new dynamic to my flying and brought a different airmanship skill altogether – the ability to self-critique and develop skills that I thought were very much set in place. Having someone say to you 'yes that is fine, but have you thought of this' can open your eyes to your inefficiencies. Being able to quickly adapt and implement feedback is a good skill to have. With this in mind, flying your mock test with someone you have never flown with will be a good learning experience for you and will also give an indication of how you deal with the pressure on the day of your skills test when you fly with, perhaps, someone you have never met before or flown with. The same applies when flying with future passengers and other qualified pilots, though this is often forgotten.

With an instructor-come-mock examiner booked, there are a couple of ground tasks that need to be completed to satisfy the pre-flight elements of the mock test. Firstly, you will need to seek out the aircraft's mass and balance sheet. Your club will have these for each of the aircraft as, unfortunately, not all aircraft weigh and behave the same despite being the same type. Though, with some thought it is rather unsurprising that over the course of many years an aircraft's mass and centre of gravity will change through maintenance and replacement of parts. Maintenance providers for the aircraft are likely to have provided the flying club with a spreadsheet in order to input payload and fuel figures, and to calculate, and display graphically, whether the aircraft will respond within its envelope. To calculate the aircraft's mass and balance, besides inputting a fuel figure, it does mean asking your mock examiner what their weight is! This may feel awkward and embarrassing, but it is a fundamental stage of your planning. Your mock examiner will be anticipating you to ask them this rather personal question.

Secondly, about a day before, your mock examiner will give you a route to plan. This route will include three points and will not be a route you have flown before, but may include previous turning points. Before getting airborne, your mock examiner will look to review your planning with regards to checking weather, NOTAMS and en-route calculations.

With regards to the aerial testing itself, you may possibly already be aware of what elements of the syllabus you will be tested on. The test is made up of two sub-sections: navigation and general handling. These previously mentioned areas of testing are general and can be rather ambiguous on first approach. I will endeavour to break these components down concisely, but with enough detail to allow you to put some plan of action in place to best deal with each scenario as they present themselves to you; though, this order is entirely at the discretion of your examiner.

1 – Execute and monitor the pre-advised route. Ensure you are timing your legs and revising ETAs, if necessary, as, more often than not, winds encountered en route will vary vastly from the wind components used in your calculations. Showing an intelligent appreciation and explanation of this will serve you well.

2 – You will be expected to divert to an aerodrome, landmark or town at some point on your second leg, as dictated by your instructor. Your mock examiner wants to see you establish your position, plot a direct routing (if safely possible) and provide a distance, heading and an ETA. Your instructor may be explicit in telling you where to divert to. But they may also just say they are unwell and want to land ASAP; in this scenario, it is down to you assess and identify the best diversion destination.

With the diversion out of the way, you will move onto the general handling section of the test:

3 – General handling will include steep turns and spiral dive recovery at height. This will be followed by a demonstration of stalling in various configurations – clean and full flap while straight and level and also in the landing configuration during a simulated base-to-final turn.

4 – You will also be asked to demonstrate a practise forced landing, though you are not likely to be pre-warned and, as such, the mock examiner will bring the power to idle. The importance of this demonstration is to show a quick appreciation for the checklist with regards to re-starting the engine and making the appropriate distress calls. Also, your examiner wants to see your commitment to a forced landing and picking a field as quickly as possible. More life-threatening incidents

can be avoided if you are able to commit to a forced landing whilst you still have altitude. Continually trying to re-start the engine after a first, and what should be your only, attempt will only serve to waste valuable altitude. In your navigation brief, and, perhaps, in your lessons, you will have been shown how to fly a circuit around your chosen field. In a life or death scenario, if you find a suitable field, your aim is to position yourself accordingly for a 'workable' final approach, preferably into wind, so it may mean your four-point circuit intention is forgotten. If this does happen, give an explanation – after all, in a real life scenario your goal is to get the aircraft down in an appropriate field, in a safe manner. Purposefully flying a four-point circuit, because that is what you were taught, may not be the best option in the given circumstances.

After the go-around instruction has been issued and you begin your climb away from the field, expect another 'engine failure' – this is to simulate an engine failure on take-off and will tick off another testing point. If you are lucky, the same field may still be achievable that you had previously selected. If not, remember to trim for the glide and select a suitable landing point either 30 degrees left or right of your track.

5 – Once at a suitable altitude, you will be given the famed 'foggles' to wear. In this part of the test, the mock examiner will assess your handling when flying on your instruments and will ask you to demonstrate a

180 degree, rate one turn to simulate you entering and exiting cloud.

6 – After your 'foggles' are removed you are likely to be geographically disorientated and some distance away from where you previously were. Your mock examiner will now ask you to demonstrate a position fix using your radio instruments i.e. through the use of VORs. If you are operating in an area with multiple radio navigation aids, having a rough idea where you are or, at least, where you were before you were given the 'foggles' to wear, may go some way in helping you decide what VORs to use.

7 – You will then make your way back to the aerodrome, where you will demonstrate a mixture of landing techniques. This also gives the mock examiner a good indication of your communication skills and ability to deal with other traffic in close proximity when within the circuit. The circuits could come in any combination and in any order. However, it is likely your last landing will be a short-field, full-flap landing given the time it would otherwise take to fully retract the flaps ahead of rotation in the case of a touch and go.

To inspire some confidence, the majority of the general handling skills are demonstrated in the first 10 minutes of flight: taxiing, take-off, climbing, climbing turns, levelling off, straight and level etc. The main purpose of your mock skills test is to assess your safety, decision making and identification of risks.

More officially, there are documents you will be able to find online that will give you the breakdown of the skills and abilities your mock examiner will be testing you on. If you search *Examiner Report for EASA PPL(A) Skill Test* you are bound to find the UK Civil Aviation Authority's (CAA) document. Considering that the CAA implement and test to EASA standard, this is a very useful document to consult irrespective of what European country you are learning to fly in. In the UK, this is the same document your real examiner will use on the day of your skills test.

Upon the successful completion of your mock skills test, your instructor-come-mock examiner will recommend you for the skills test. In order to maintain a level of momentum, it would be pragmatic to attempt to undertake your mock and real skills test as close as viably possible; perhaps, over the course of a weekend, weather conditions permitting. Your club will likely encourage such planning. After all, your mock test, if successful, will be your last flight before your skills test with the approved examiner. Naturally, if you 'fail' your mock test, your instructor will provide the necessary feedback on techniques and procedures that require attention. These areas of weakness will likely be addressed in an one-hour revision lesson before a second attempt at the mock test.

In terms of dealing with your pre-test nerves, the skills test itself is unlikely to differ from your mock test in terms of structure and the elements of the syllabus you will be tested on. That should, in turn, help to settle any pre-test jitters – as you are not likely to face something you have not already practised or, at the very least, been briefed on. A concern of mine, ahead of my skills test, was how I was going to get on with the examiner. I did not meet my examiner until the day of my test; owing to the schedule I wanted to work to, the club had to contract an external examiner in from a different flying club. The first time we spoke was, in fact, only the night before the test so I could be briefed on the route and ask for the relative information to calculate my mass and balance figures. My concern was based around the insecurity that, perhaps, we would not develop a good relationship and this would affect my performance detrimentally during the test. As it happened, this insecurity came unfounded, as the examiner and I hit it off immediately when we were introduced in the morning. Remember, never under-estimate the influence of relationships in the cockpit.

Regarding the briefing phone call the night before, it does not leave you much time to organise yourself and prepare mentally. It may go without saying, but in the evening before your skills test find yourself a quiet work space where you are able to prepare adequately. Owing to how infrequent we fly, especially during the training period, it is unlikely you have a streamlined, fool-proof checklist or preparation procedure. Unless you are super organised, I am sure there is always at least one item you have arrived to your previous lessons without. Perhaps, this could even be something as trivial as your sunglasses or a pen. Despite how much you may try to underplay your nerves and jitters on the day, there will certainly be an element of exhilaration and adrenaline as your impending test draws near. Such emotions can lead to distractions, oversights and mistakes. So while you are still relatively relaxed, ensure in good time you have all the necessary equipment already packed. This equipment list should include your diversion ruler; flight computer; VFR chart; checklist; semi-permanent maker pens; a time-keeping device and finally a writing space to record your in-flight notes and journey log. Situations wherein you are asked to calculate the distance to a diversion are more easily managed when you have the right equipment!

Administratively, there are preparations to be made. Your club will have on file your training record and all other documents, such as your ground theory examination results and radiotelephony oral examination documents. For the purpose of inspection, these will be made available to the examiner. Your club should have a copy of your Class 1 or 2 medical certificate on file – however, for the purpose of inspection, the authority-approved examiner will require the original. A good pilot should always carry their medical certificate when flying, but a worrying amount of pilots I have met do not.

In relation to the planning of your flight, there is very little you can do the evening before in terms of calculations. What you can do, however, is draw the route, measure the distances and tracks and begin filling in the route journey log. This will be a route that you would not have flown before point-to-point, but many of the areas you will transit through you would have undoubtedly operated in. So be sure to cast your eye over your VFR chart for obstacles, areas to avoid such as dangers or restricted areas. Also, pay attention to wildlife areas such as bird sanctuaries. Whilst these areas are not restricted or structurally defined in terms of boundary and altitude, it is in the name of responsible airmanship to plan around such areas.

With good planning, the only tasks you will need to undertake on the day will be the route calculations based on weather and the checking of NOTAMs.

Whilst plenty of attention is given to your planning in the days leading up to your skills test, you must make sure you give yourself adequate attention and consideration, also. You may produce an outstanding brief for your examiner, but if you have stayed up all night and have not eaten in the hours leading up to your test, your hard work may be in vain in the instance your performance lets you down. If you complete your prep work in a timely fashion, put it aside and focus on ensuring you are fit and ready for your flight. A minor calculation error in your planning can be forgiven, a flight safety issue as a result of fatigue or being unfit for flight cannot. In light of this, in the days leading up to your test make sure you eat a balanced diet, keeping hydrated and certainly avoiding alcohol. With good physiological preparation, you are likely to present yourself for test in good form with sharp and sound alertness. The benefits of such preparation also reflect in your psychology and you will feel mentally prepared. Transversely, if you are not feeling physically or mentally prepared, perhaps owing to sickness or lack of sleep, it would be shrewd to look into delaying your test.

During the test itself, I am almost certain that by the time you sit in the cockpit and are working through your checklists, any feelings of nerves will subside in order for you to focus on the task in hand. During the navigation phase at the beginning of the test, there will be ample opportunity to enter conversation with your examiner – this should relax you into a calmer state of mind. Soon into the test, you will realise that this skills test is not a fast-paced drill exercise where the examiner is looking to fail you or catch you out. Rather, it is a safety assessment of your performance. So long as you can demonstrate over the entire flight you are in control, you are monitoring your progress and that you have an awareness of safety issues, then you are certainly heading in the right direction for a pass. Flying to an exact altitude and following a heading precisely is not the objective of the test. My examiner explained that many students fixate on their flying accuracy but reiterated that quite frankly at this level of flying it is the safety awareness they are looking to see demonstrated. Being able to hold a heading and follow a track without correction is impressive, they said, but a good pilot, in their eyes, is one who can unintentionally depart from their track, identify their deviation in a timely fashion and subsequently apply a solution. This statement certainly made me reconsider my definition of a good pilot.

With good preparation, and a small amount of luck, you will have passed your skills test! However long it has taken for you to get to this stage, all of a sudden there will be a sense of great relief. Whilst flying is incredibly fun, working towards something as monumental as a PPL does bring an element of pressure and strain. This can be measured in both personal and financial terms. After all, the day of your test will likely be the most expensive day of flying yet as it is likely to include two hours of flying, the skills test fee and also the submission of your PPL application form that can cost from £150-£200 (165-220 €*). However, that aside, to finally achieve this goal is a true test and representation of your character.

The champagne must wait a little while longer, though. For, unfortunately, soon after comes more paper work. Ironically, it was this element that proved to be one of the most testing parts of the PPL for me. So, in that respect, I would advise you to settle your excitement until you have sent off your paper work for processing

---

*   Exchange rate £1 = 1.10 € (Winter 2018)

by your national aviation authority. You must make sure that your paperwork is entirely correct and completed. In my excitement and determination to get home to spread the news, I failed to complete two elements of my application. One was a signature and the other was the card payment information to pay for the licence. This resulted in my club having to forward my paper work to my address 200 miles away, once they had spotted the mistake, for me to then fill in the relevant fields and dispatch it from my home address to the aviation authority. This mistake probably held up the issue of my PPL by about a week.

You can see the importance, and consequence, of not filling in the paper work correctly.

G iven that it may take up to, or beyond, a month for you to receive your licence, I feel obliged to continue with my guide until you have the PPL physically in your hand. This chapter can be seen as an encore, if you will, and is planned to be a thought-provoking topic, regarding how best to proceed with your flying. You will recall, in an earlier chapter, options on how to develop your future flying were discussed. These options included the Night and Instrument Ratings, as well as setting goals for your flying. However, this chapter will take a look at options and decisions regarding your access to flight – whether through your club membership, a share in an aircraft or some other means.

While your licence is being processed by your aviation authority, your access to flying is somewhat restricted until your licence is in your possession. However, you can still fly solo, and any hours built during this period can be recorded as pilot-in-command hours. They will need to be authorised by an instructor and you will not be able to take passengers during this period. This procedure differs in no way to how your instructor once authorised you to fly solo as a student. I suppose it is in this period when you may now, as a qualified pilot, look at other options to further your flying. In this situation, where you are still being signed off by your instructor, it may feel as though you are still a student. With your qualification gained, you may want to give some consideration to, perhaps, seeking out a new flying adventure and base that better suits your circumstances. Understandably, at this time, you may feel indebted to your club. After all, through their tutelage you have become a pilot. I would advise in this period, between passing your skills test and your licence arriving, giving some thought to how to maximise your flying time, both financially and in terms of access.

The options available to you at this juncture are the following:

1 – Remain with the club you trained with.
2 – Move to a different club.
3 – Buy an equity share in an aircraft.
4 – Join a non-equity flying group.

I have been deliberately vague in order to adequately break down the pros and cons of each option.

Opting to remain with your current club is the zero hassle option. You will be familiar with the aircraft, the airfield operation and would have already developed relationships within the club which will, perhaps, make it easier to fly with other pilots. Another advantage of staying with your club is having access to instructors and their knowledge. It will be easier to organise check-rides and undertake further training should you look to.

On the other hand, choosing to remain with your club may also have its disadvantages. To start with, you may not be getting the best per-hour rate available. You may find other clubs in the area may offer better deals to their qualified members. Another factor, briefly referenced earlier, is that you may not feel like you have become a fully-fledged pilot. This may not apply, but once you have your licence it may be beneficial to experience a change of scenery. Staying at the same club may leave you feeling like you are still a student. Having a fresh new start elsewhere, wherever that may be, might be the catalyst in kick-starting your independent flying.

Moving to a different club may be a good option if cost is an influential and deciding factor in your selection making. As mentioned just before, it may work out cheaper to fly at a new club. Much like the club you trained at, you will still benefit from having access to an instructor and will be able to undertake further training. If one of your goals is to fly new aircraft, then moving to a new club that has a diverse and varied fleet may assist in achieving this objective.

By moving to a new club, it may mean you have to operate out of a new airfield. If this is the case, note that you will likely have to undertake a couple of introductory flights with an instructor to introduce you to the local area and airfield procedure. To that end, moving to a new airfield soon after gaining your licence may impact your confidence. If you think you may benefit from taking small and gradual steps after the issue of your licence, suddenly changing your surroundings may not be the best option for you. Also, you are unlikely to have many relationships at a new club which may make integrating a little difficult. Also, be mindful of hidden costs. In Chapter four, membership and landing fees were discussed. With that considered, be sure to assess all costs fully. A way to sensibly assess a potential move is to break down all costs and work out what your 'true' per hour cost is over a realistic amount of flying hours. In most instances, if you pay a membership fee you will tend to benefit from better hourly rates. However, that is only the case if you are flying a lot of hours. See my example below:

For 10 hours of flying*:

Club A - £150 per hr x 10hrs = £1,500
Club B - £145 per hr x 10hrs + £100 membership fee = £1,550.

For 30 hours of flying:

Club A - £150 per hr x 30hrs = £4,500
Club B - £145 per hr x 30hrs + £100 membership fee =£4,450

These crude calculations suggest that flying at a club with a higher hourly rate, but without a membership fee, will be more cost effective if you are flying in the region of 10 hours. Naturally, if that increases towards 30 hours of flying, it would be more astute to pay for a membership at the second club.

Moving away from a club environment, an alternative means to access an aircraft is through owning a share. To own an aircraft outright would involve a huge financial up-front cost, so many

---

* Exchange rate £1 = 1.10 € (Winter 2018)

pilots elect to own a share in an aircraft. Even the most basic, second-hand aircraft can cost around £20,000-£30,000. With that in mind, it lessens the financial burden to joint-own an aircraft with other members.

The advantages of owning a share in an aircraft is that access to the aircraft will be more attainable. In a club environment, you may have 20 people a week looking to book out the aircraft for one-hour slots. If you own a share in an aircraft, only others who also own a share will be able to fly it. Share proportions tend to average between one-quarter to one-tenth shares. Naturally, the bigger the share, the fewer people in the consortium. So, if you own a one-sixth share, only five others will have access to it, meaning it will be far easier to book out the aircraft for an entire day or weekend. A further advantage of owning the share is the lower per-hour rate. Unlike a club who look to maximise revenue, in a shared ownership, your hourly rate is likely to be largely for fuel.

However, there are some disadvantages to consider when assessing this option. Foremost, you will only have access to one aircraft; should you wish to fly a different aircraft you may have to revert to one of the previously discussed options to gain more experience on alternative types. As previously mentioned, the large up-front cost is the main issue to contend with if you are considering this option. Even towards the cheap end of the spectrum, share prices often begin at around £3,000 (3,300 €*). However, besides

---

* Exchange rate £1 = 1.10 € (Winter 2018)

that initial cost, in a shared ownership scheme, you will also be expected to a pay a monthly fee for various up-keep costs such as a maintenance fund, insurance, hangarage, airfield fees and any other miscellaneous costs associated with the ownership of an aircraft. Further disadvantages are the financial exposure to repairs and servicing of the aircraft that fall solely on the group members. Despite paying a monthly fee to cover maintenance costs, any work required that cannot be covered by the maintenance fund will need to be fronted by the members. This, naturally, brings us towards the political issues that may arise through a shared-ownership venture. Disagreements may arise through decisions that need to be made within the group concerning the aircraft. Examples could include disputes over relocating the aircraft to a new airfield or looking to explore cheaper options in response to a repair scenario. Also, divisions may arise if one member flies the aircraft more than others; which may lead to conversations over the equality of monthly payments from members. Furthermore, in the instance that a member decides to leave the shared ownership, the preferred outcome would be for the individual to sell on their share to another prospective member. However, in certain circumstances, it may be the case that the remaining members absorb that share. As a result, you as a remaining member will be expected to pay an equal division of the share back to the departing member and pick up additional monthly costs. It could be the case you owned a one-sixth share to begin with and by the end of your ownership you own a one-quarter share, which will mean an increase in monthly costs. Whilst you will own more of the aircraft, your share value will naturally depreciate with the age and condition of the aircraft.

If you were to treat your initial share cost as an investment and removed it from the equation, your monthly running cost, coupled with your cheaper per hour rate, may work out to be comparable with the cost of flying at a club. The risk is the value of your share decreasing, coupled with being exposed to extortionate maintenance and repair costs – factors that are you are not burdened with if you fly at a club. For a low-hour pilot looking to build hours on a budget, I would not recommend this option. If you were a hobby pilot with some cash set aside, then this option, perhaps, may suit your circumstances.

The final option to consider is a non-equity group. A non-equity group is an aircraft, or a fleet of aircraft, that is owned by an external party. This means that as non-equity group member, you will have no exposure to organising maintenance, repairs and other running costs. Unlike a flying club or school, the focus is less on maximising income. As such, members will pay a small monthly cost to cover the same costs highlighted in the shared-ownership scheme. The lesser monthly cost is balanced out by more members in the group, perhaps around 20 per aircraft. Similar to the shared-ownership option, the per-hour rate tends to be substantially less than the rates offered by flying clubs. If the group has more than one aircraft or type to offer, then this can be substantially more attractive than owning a share in a single aircraft.

As ever, I will provide some disadvantages of becoming involved in such a group. These groups are able to offer affordable prices because of the size of their membership. This does mean, however, that access to flying may be limited due to sheer demand of the aircraft. Many private pilots looking to undertake commercial training will look to complete their hour-building through such a group. This means that you may very well find booking the aircraft for a one-hour slot difficult because another party has booked the aircraft for three lots of two-hour slots throughout the week, on the days you were looking to fly. Another disadvantage, in relation to the availability of access, is the wear and tear of the aircraft. Whilst you are not responsible for the up-keep of the aircraft, owing to how often these aircraft fly, you may find that the aircraft may have minor defects and serviceability issues. I once flew as a passenger with a friend who was a member in a group and the aircraft they were looking to fly had an unserviceable attitude indicator. For the purpose of VFR flight, this was not an issue that was going to ground the aircraft. However, the rectification was planned to be deferred until the aircraft's 50-hour check, which was still 27 flight hours away. Naturally, this meant all pilots who would fly the aircraft after us would experience the same defect. However, if some of those pilots held an Instrument Rating (Restricted) and were looking to fly in more marginal en-route conditions, in which circumstances the attitude indicator is required, this would effectively limit their opportunity to do so until the defect had been addressed.

My opinion for a low-hour pilot, fresh from their PPL training, would be to stay with your club for a little while after you have your PPL and build some confidence, then look around for a better deal at a different club which may offer you more diversity in terms of the aircraft you will be able to fly – try a new type, for example.

If you are looking to hour-build in order to undertake commercial training, bypass a second club and seek out a non-equity flying group, which will offer you the savings for the more hours you fly. If, however, you are a happy hobby pilot then remain with your club. If you have little interest in flying other types and you are able appreciate and assess the risk, then, perhaps, consider an aircraft share. However, I would only ever advise this if you have the financial stability to do so. You do not want to find yourself in a position where your lifestyle is impeded in order to prioritise costs towards an aircraft that you will only fly once a month.

ACKNOWLEDGEMENTS

T he idea to begin writing this book developed in early 2018 during a quiet shift. It served as a distraction while I was unable to take regular flying lessons. Over the course of that summer I was able to complete my flying licence and this period greatly inspired the completion of this book.

I would like to acknowledge and thank TG Aviation of Kent. In particular, I thank Sue and Mark Girdler who managed and directed my training. This also extends to their daughters Tasha and Sophie. The Girdlers are a formidable aviation family and I owe a lot of where I am today to their passion for flying and their commitment to high flight training and safety standards. Also, thank you to my instructors Craig and Steve who were my staple tutors throughout this period. Also, to Andy who flew my mock test with me. Though we never flew together, Gary Merchant was always on hand to guide and nurture my development. It was his assured words back in January 2018 that confirmed my decision to move away from my club and begin a career in airline operations. I also want to acknowledge his hard work through the Nick Davidson Memorial Trust scholarships that has provided aviation opportunities to young, aspiring aviators.

I extend my thanks to my employer, whose identity I have chosen to withhold in this publication. Much of what I have learned in my time in their operations department has influenced this book. I am grateful for the time and resources they have allowed me to complete this work.

I want to acknowledge the understanding and patience of Matt Falcus and DestinWorld Publishing while I wrote this book. Life can get in the way and, at times, this has hindered the progress of this book.

To my supportive and understanding girlfriend Chloe, I give my thanks. I would not have the opportunities I have now without her support. From moving away with me to understanding how important I regard my flying, she has been a supportive force.

Finally, and most importantly, I want to acknowledge my family; in particular, my Mum and Dad as well as my older brothers, James and Samuel. Thank you for all the experiences we have shared, I am a true believer the people we are today owes itself to the people we were yesterday. I will always strive to make you proud and will always look to act in your best interests.

BIBLIOGRAPHY

Trevor Thom, *The Air Pilot's Manual 1: Flying Training* (Air Pilot Publishing, 2018)

Trevor Thom, *The Air Pilot's Manual 2: Air Law & Meteorology* (Air Pilot Publishing, 2017)

Trevor Thom, *The Air Pilot's Manual 3: Navigation* (Air Pilot Publishing, 2018)

Trevor Thom, *The Air Pilot's Manual 4: The Aeroplane – Technical* (Air Pilot Publishing, 2017)

Trevor Thom, *The Air Pilot's Manual 5: Radio Navigation & Instrument Flying* (Air Pilot Publishing, 2018)

Trevor Thom, *The Air Pilot's Manual 6: Human Performances & Operational Procedures* (Air Pilot Publishing, 2017)

Trevor Thom, *The Air Pilot's Manual 7: Communications* (Air Pilot Publishing, 2017)

R. D. Campbell, *Ground Handling For The Private Pilot Licence* (Collins, 1981)

Pooleys, *Pooleys Flight Guide United Kingdom 56th Edition* (Pooleys, 2018)

E. H. J. Pallet, *Aircraft Instruments and Integrated Systems* (Longman, 1992)

REFERENCES

University of Nebraska, *Height Distribution of Birds Recorded by Collisions with Civil Aircraft*
http://digitalcommons.unl.edu/cgi/viewcontent.
cgi?article=1496&context=icwdm_usdanwrc (2006)

EASA, *EGAST Radiotelephony Guide for VFR Pilots*
https://www.easa.europa.eu/sites/default/files/dfu/EGAST_Radiotelephony-guide-for-VFR-pilots.pdf (2010)

ICAO, *Annex 5 -Units of Measurements to be Used in Air and Ground Operations*
https://aerosavvy.com/wp-content/uploads/2014/08/an05_cons.pdf (2010)

ICAO, *TheManual of Radiotelephony Doc 943*
http://dgca.gov.in/intradgca/intra/icaodocs/Doc%20
9432%20-%20Manual%20Radiotelephony%20Ed%204%20
(En).pdf (2007)

ICAO, *Abbreviations and Codes Doc 8400*
http://www1.atmb.net.cn/CD_web/
UploadFile/201305281O480238.pdf (2010)